EMPERORS IN IMAGES, ARCHITECTURE, AND RITUAL: AUGUSTUS TO FAUSTA

T0126306

SELECTED PAPERS
ON ANCIENT ART AND ARCHITECTURE

SERIES EDITOR
MIREILLE M. LEE

NUMBER 5
Emperors in Images, Architecture, and Ritual

EMPERORS IN IMAGES, ARCHITECTURE, AND RITUAL: AUGUSTUS TO FAUSTA

edited by
Francesco de Angelis

Archaeological Institute of America
Boston, MA
2020

EMPERORS IN IMAGES, ARCHITECTURE, AND RITUAL: AUGUSTUS TO FAUSTA

ISBN 978-1-948488-64-8

Cover design by Susanne Wilhelm. Cover image: Detail of Sarcophagus lid fragment with quadriga and youth, marble, 300–350 C.E. (© The Trustees of the British Museum 1805,0703.145 / Art Resource, NY ART556088).

Library of Congress Cataloging-in-Publication Data

Names: Angelis, Francesco de, 1968- editor. | Archaeological Institute of
    America, issuing body.
Title: Emperors in images, architecture, and ritual : Augustus to Fausta /
    edited by Francesco de Angelis.
Description: Boston, MA : Archaeological Institute of America, 2020. |
    Series: Selected papers on ancient art and architecture ; number 5 |
    Includes bibliographical references.
Identifiers: LCCN 2020052177 | ISBN 9781948488648 (paperback)
Subjects: LCSH: Emperors--Rome--Portraits. | Emperor worship--Rome. |
    Rome--Religion.
Classification: LCC N7588 .E47 2020 | DDC 704.9/48--dc23
LC record available at https://lccn.loc.gov/2020052177

Printed in the United States on acid-free paper.

Contents

Tensa or Triumphal Chariot? The Iconography of (Some) Empty Chariots on Roman Imperial Coins

Jacob A. Latham

Abstract

A series of coins with enigmatic images of empty chariots were minted from Augusts to Titus. Who or what did these vehicles convey? And in what context? A careful and systematic comparison of these mysterious vehicles with other quadrigae that represent a triumph yields some clear and distinct iconographical differences. The evidence suggests that these obscure, empty chariots were in fact tensae, *sacred chariots that carried the symbols of the gods to the circus, employed as a synecdoche for the* pompa circensis *and the circus games that followed.*

FROM AUGUSTUS TO TITUS, IMPERIAL MONEYERS MINTED a series of coins with enigmatic images of empty chariots— typically *quadrigae* if the horse train was represented. Similar, though iconographically distinct, *quadrigae* appeared on *denarii* minted in 87 B.C.E. by Lucius Rubrius Dossenus. Standard numismatic corpora, both print and digital, regularly describe these cars as triumphal or, more cautiously, as slow (their horses appear to be walking) or pacing ornamented *quadrigae*. For example, *Coins of the Roman Empire in the British Museum* describes figure 1 as a "triumphal quadriga r., horses pacing; the car is ornamented with figures at front and side and is surmounted by four miniature galloping horses."[1] But who or what did these vehicles convey, if anything? And in what context? Were they, in fact, triumphal or something else? A comparison of these mysterious cars with other numismatic representations of more obviously triumphal chariots highlights distinct iconography and so suggests distinct vehicles. So, if these empty chariots are not specifically triumphal, what are they?

A comparison with other visual sources offers some assistance. Imperial imagery in other media, namely, marble reliefs, show architecturally or structurally similar chariots, but with attendants. These attendants may be *pueri patrimi et matrimi*, boys both of whose parents were still living, and/or *tensarii*, ritual technicians, both of whom are known, from textual evidence, to have accompanied *tensae*, sacred vehicles in which sat *exuviae*, the symbols or relics of the gods, as they traversed the city in a *pompa circensis*, the procession that inaugurated the chariot races. Though the triumph was assuredly one of Rome's greatest spectacles, it was not the only one. Moreover, these other spectacles were also important in the construction and representation of imperial authority. In the end, the enigmatic chariots may be *tensae* and their images may have served as a synecdoche for the *pompa circensis* and the games that followed.

Comparing Numismatic Iconography

A careful and systematic comparison of numismatic images of these enigmatic vehicles with other *quadrigae* also characterized as triumphal yields some clear and distinct iconographical differences. The reverse of an *aureus* minted under Octavian in 32–29 B.C.E. depicts an empty chariot pulled to the right by four horses walking in step (fig. 1).[2] Figural designs adorn the front and side of the chariot, while four miniature horses leap from a triangular pediment. The legend names Caesar son of a god—that is, Octavian who appears on the obverse—who may be the recipient of this chariot or, better, its patron. A contemporaneous *denarius* symbolizes Octavian's triumph over Cleopatra—and Mark Antony, of course—at the battle of Actium. The obverse shows a winged Victory, standing on the prow of a ship, clutching a branch in her left hand and holding out a crown with her right. On the reverse, a crowned Octavian, "Caesar son of a god," drives what may be called a "triumphal" chariot with ornamented sides, as he extends a branch in his right hand and grasps the reins with his left (fig. 2).[3]

Though similar in some respects—both sport figural decoration and something like a footboard at the back for a driver to mount the chariot—the *quadrigae* display some clear differences.[4] Most prominently, the "triumphal" chariot on the *denarius* has a "triumphantly" attired driver. Equally importantly, their "architecture," as it were, differs: the triumphal chariot on the *denarius* is curvilinear, rounded even, with a gently sloping flat-top, and is nearly equal in height to its horse train, while the *triumphator* towers above. By contrast, the empty chariot on the *aureus* is rectilinear, almost boxy, with a pediment—a key iconographical difference—that towers above its horse train.[5] Even the curved rear side, which suggests a mounting platform, differs between the two sets of coins: swooping vigorously behind Augustus, but more gradually on the empty chariot.

A comparison of later Augustan coinage yields similar results. A *denarius* minted in 18 B.C.E. and now in the British Museum—whose near twin from the same mint supposedly "alludes in general to triumphs of Augustus"—shows another tall, boxy chariot with a mounting platform in back and a pediment in front, at whose apex four horses gallop, with a winged Victory (perhaps) on the side and an aquila, a staff surmounted by an eagle possibly representing the recently reacquired standards from Parthia, inside (fig. 3).[6] By contrast, the reverse of an *aureus* from 13–14 C.E. has a laurel-crowned Tiberius, with a laurel branch in his right hand and an eagle-tipped scepter in his left, standing in a low, rounded, gently sloping, flat-topped chariot with no visible decoration and, interestingly, no footboard despite the presence of a driver.[7] An aquila in the otherwise empty chariot suggests a triumphal honor, though the chariot unquestionably differs from the more self-evident *currus triumphalis* that Tiberius rides as he clutches his own aquila standard.

The empty *quadriga* with an aquila has been identified with yet another contemporary empty chariot from the same Spanish mint.[8] Under a tetrastyle-domed structure stands a so-called "triumphal currus" with a footboard at the back, decoration on the side, a galloping *quadriga* on top, and an aquila within (fig. 4).[9] The footboard, miniature *quadriga*, and aquila does not, however, mean that they are the same

Fig. 1. Empty quadriga *surmounted by four horses,* aureus *of Augustus (Octavian), 32–29 B.C.E., Rome/Brindisi? (BPK Bildagentur / Münzkabinett, Staatliche Museen, Berlin 18202357 / Dirk Sonnenwald / Art Resource, NY ART502983).*

Fig. 2. Octavian in a triumphal quadriga, denarius *of Augustus (Octavian), 32–29 B.C.E., Rome/Brindisi? (© The Trustees of the British Museum R.6163 / Art Resource, NY ART556082).*

3

Fig. 3. *Empty* quadriga *with an aquila,* denarius, 18 B.C.E. of Augustus, Colonia Patricia? (© The Trustees of the British Museum 1844,0425.427 / Art Resource, NY ART556087).

Fig. 4. *Empty chariot under a tetrastyle dome,* denarius, 18 B.C.E. of Augustus, Colonia Patricia? (BPK Bildagentur / Münzkabinett, Staatliche Museen, Berlin 18202558 / Art Resource, NY ART556028).

vehicle. To judge from the standard, the chariot under the dome appears shorter, has a flat top without a pediment, and a rounded front much like the triumphal chariot driven by Tiberius. By contrast, the *quadriga* in figure 3 seems taller, rectilinear, and has a pediment. In other words, though both coins were minted at the same time, at the same mint, and show empty chariots with a footboard, miniature galloping horses and an aquila, the chariots do not look the same, which suggests that they are not, in fact, the same vehicle. It is important to note that figure 3 from the British Museum differs significantly from other exemplars of the "same" coin type, which do in fact cohere closely to the iconography of the empty chariot with an aquila under the dome. In fact, it would seem that the *RIC* lumped a series of tall, boxy, vertically oriented empty chariots with figural ornamentation (Victory perhaps) together with similar, but visually distinct, low, rounded, and horizontally oriented vehicles decorated with abstract scrollwork.[10]

Subsequent coin issues reveal a similar contrast. An *aureus* minted under Nero in 54 C.E. shows the now-familiar tall, boxy empty *quadriga*, now with Victories flanking the four miniature acroterial horses and EX S C in the exergue indicating senatorial ratification of the apotheosis of *Divus Claudius Augustus*, who appears on the obverse (fig. 5).[11] Unlike Augustan versions of this vehicle, the Neronian *quadriga* shows no footboard and so no platform for a driver. A *sestertius* minted almost 20 years earlier under Tiberius (35–36 C.E.) also depicts a tall, rider-less chariot, but, on the better-preserved examples, a second curved line at the top of the parapet-like superstructure suggests cylindrical architecture—much like the chariot driven by Tiberius on the Augustan coin (see fig. 2).[12] Moreover, it is flat-topped and rounded much like the chariot in the tetrastyle domed temple (see fig. 4).

Later still, Titus honored his deified father, Vespasian, with the last extant example of this enigmatic chariot, which *Roman Imperial Coinage* describes as a "slow quadriga … with the car in [the] form of [a] small, richly ornamented temple, surmounted by two Victories" (fig. 6).[13] Like the *quadriga* dedicated to Claudius, deified Vespasian's chariot also has Victories flanking the miniature quadriga on the pediment, figural decoration on its façade and side, and EX S C in the exergue to signal senatorial approval of the divinization of *Divus Augustus Vespasianus*, who appears on the obverse. Similarly, Vespasian's chariot lacks a mounting platform or footboard. A near-contemporary *aureus* shows Vespasian on what is unquestionably a triumphal chariot—the bound captive, soldier, trumpeter, and Victory crowning the emperor are explicitly glossed as a triumph by the legend TRIVMP AVG (fig. 7).[14] Like the triumphal chariot in which Octavian stands (fig. 2), or the empty quadriga under the dome (fig. 4), the *currus triumphalis* of Vespasian swoops low, standing shorter than its horse train with a gently sloping, flat top, and a rounded or curvilinear shape. In the end, numismatic iconography clearly and consistently distinguished the tall and boxy empty *quadrigae* (with or without a footboard) with a pediment from either the tall and cylindrical or the low and swooping triumphal chariots.

Fig. 5. Empty quadriga *surmounted by horses and Victories, aureus of Nero, 54 C.E., Rome (BPK Bildagentur / Münzkabinett, Staatliche Museen, Berlin 18203214 / Lutz-Jürgen Lübke / Art Resource, NY ART500217).*

Identifying the Enigmatic, Empty Chariot

Such distinctions suggest these enigmatic, empty *quadrigae* are not in fact triumphal chariots. So what are they? Stefan Weinstock and John Rich have both argued that the chariots minted under Augustus, at least, represent triumphal honors specifically for that emperor. Carsten Lange maintains that the Augustan chariots are a kind of hybrid between a *tensa* (processional wagon) and triumphal chariot and so signal deification. Such arguments, however, do not seem to account for the clear similarities between the Augustan *quadrigae* and Claudius's and Vespasian's. All four markedly rectilinear chariots tower above their horse trains and sport similar, but not the same, acroterial decoration springing from the pedi-

Fig. 6. Empty quadriga *surmounted by Victories holding crowns,* aureus *of Titus, 80–81 C.E., Rome (© The Trustees of the British Museum 1864,1128.254 / Art Resource, NY ART556086).*

Fig. 7. Vespasian in a triumphal quadriga, aureus *of Vespasian, 71 C.E., Rome (© The Trustees of the British Museum 1864,1128.255 / Art Resource, NY ART556026).*

ment, suggesting that the footboard on the Augustan variants may be an acceptable deviation from an otherwise standard type (figs. 1, 3, 5, and 6). In fact, Augustus himself was honored with a tall, boxy empty chariot—though not on coinage until the civil wars after the death of Nero.[15] Its clear resemblance to the chariots of deified Claudius and Vespasian—a flat back without a footboard, a clearly discernible pediment surmounted by a *quadriga* flanked by Victories, and the legend in the exergue, EX S C—suggests that the obverse shows not just a son of a god signaled by the legend AVGVSTVS DIVI F, but a god in his own right—the deified Augustus, son of the deified Caesar.

The striking iconographic similarities strongly suggest, but only suggest, that all of these chariots represent the same type of vehicle—and so also the same type of honor. If all these chariots represent the same honor granted to every deified autocrat from Caesar to Vespasian, then what specifically is the chariot? The honor would seem to be deification as may be discerned most readily from the *aurei*, which explicitly depict the deified Claudius (DIVVS CLAVDIVS AVGVSTVS) and Vespasian (DIVVS AVGVSTVS VESPASIANVS) on their observes and signal senatorial approval (EX S C) on their reverses. The *denarius* from 68–69 C.E. similarly features Augustus on the obverse and senatorial approval on the reverse, but the obverse legend names Augustus as son of a god, not deified Augustus himself, much like the *aureus* from 32–29 B.C.E. which names Caesar (that is, Octavian) son of

a god, rather than deified Julius Caesar (fig. 1). Only the *de-narius* from Spain (CAESARI AVGVSTO on the obverse, and S P Q R on the reverse) fails to reference a *divus* (fig. 3). The Augustan chariots, whether minted under Augustus or in honor of Augustus, thus differ slightly from the chariots of Claudius and Vespasian in terms of iconography (the mounting platform at the back) and the inscriptions, which obliquely name the honoree. Even so, it would seem that this temple-like chariot was a postmortem honor, a sign or symbol of the deification of the deceased—whether Caesar, Augustus, Claudius, or Vespasian.

As it turns out, the chariot in honor of Augustus may be represented in other media. A fragment of an extensive, but largely lost marble relief cycle from the mid-first century C.E., which might have belonged to a monumental altar or imperial cult sanctuary, features the familiar tall, boxy, empty chariot with a pediment but without a footboard, followed by, at least, two *togati* wearing laurel wreaths, one of whom holds a laurel branch (fig. 8).[16] An eagle perches on the pediment, below which Aeneas carries his father on his shoulder while leading his son by the hand. Romulus, perhaps carrying a trophy, graces the side. The Vergilian echoes of the iconography, which resonate well with the clear references to Actium on

Fig. 8. Relief with quadriga and two attendants, marble, mid-first century C.E. (© Szépművészeti Múzeum, Budapest #2000.24.A; photograph by László Mátyus, 2015).

7

Fig. 9. Sarcophagus lid fragment with quadriga *and youth, marble, 300–350 C.E. (© The Trustees of the British Museum 1805,0703.145 / Art Resource, NY ART556088) .*

other related reliefs, compellingly points to a monument in honor of Augustus.

Similar vehicles appear on two fourth-century C.E. marble reliefs. One early fourth-century relief seems to represent a chariot in honor of Augustus, whose decorative scheme however differs from the first-century "Actium" relief.[17] This early fourth-century relief shows a similar tall, boxy chariot with a pediment and without a footboard, accompanied by four *togati*, one of whom appears to be a young man looking back at the chariot. The Capitoline triad or perhaps the imperial genius flanked by Roma and Victory adorn the façade, while the side sports what may be Augustus' *corona civica* flanked by two laurel trees. A second early fourth-century relief from a sarcophagus lid represents another (relatively) tall, boxy *quadriga* with a pediment and without a mounting platform accompanied by a young man, who also looks back toward the chariot (fig. 9).[18] Jupiter holding a staff in his right hand and a scepter in his left adorns the façade, while on the long side the Dioscuri stand shoulder to shoulder holding reins with one hand and staffs with the other.

The *quadrigae* on these three marble reliefs bear a strong resemblance to the numismatic images: all of the chariots are tall (rising above the heads of the horse train), rectilinear in shape, with a pediment and no footboard—except on the coins minted under Augustus. The shared iconography suggests that all of these images, whether coin or marble, represent the same, or a similar, type of vehicle. If so, then the attendants on the reliefs may offer some insight into its identity and use.

It is possible, though not ultimately provable, that the young male attendants represent *pueri patrimi et matrimi* in their role as ritual attendants of *tensae*, "sacred vehicles" that were used almost exclusively in the *pompa circensis*, the religious procession before chariot races.[19] In this procession, *tensae* carried the *exuviae*, symbols or relics of the gods, who were also represented by anthropomorphic statues borne on *fercula* or litters in the parade. Unfortunately, there are no extant descriptions of the form of a *tensa*: Sinnius Capito, as noted by Verrius Flaccus via Festus, merely indicated that it was made of ivory and silver.[20] Even so, the *tensae* seem to have had a number of ritual attendants, including a *puer patrimus et matrimus*, who needed to hold to his *tensa*, maintaining contact, and to not let a rein slip to avoid a ritual fault.[21] In fact, Fabio Guidetti has argued that the laurel branch touching the *tensa*, if that is what it is, on the mid-first-century C.E. relief and the oddly flowing cape of the boy in the second early fourth-century relief may visually represent this ritual taboo (figs. 8 and 9).[22] These young men maintain contact, even if mediated, with their chariot. Admittedly, the young man in the first early fourth-century relief makes only visual contact with his *tensa*. Even so, these young or younger male attendants may be *pueri patrimi et matrimi* accompanying their *tensae*.

The other figures on the reliefs may be *tensarii*, ritual attendants of *tensae* whose possible existence is attested by a single passage from Accius (ca. 170–86 B.C.E.), later quoted by Nonius Marcellus (fourth–fifth centuries C.E.), which notes that "some of them fit bridles to the *tensa* and to the mouths of the horses."[23] It would seem, then, that there were specific individuals who took care of the horse train of the *tensae* and so would be reasonably represented alongside the boy with both parents living who need to maintain contact with the chariot. Or, perhaps the additional figures are *nomenclatores tensarum*, officials who guided the horses and announced the identity of the occupant of the *tensa*—an office attested to by a single inscription on an late second-century C.E. altar to Sol Invictus.[24]

In addition to the attendants, the figural imagery on the relief-chariots supports, albeit tenuously, their identification as *tensae*. The Capitoline triad of Jupiter flanked by Juno and Minerva, or possibly the imperial genius flanked by Roma and Victory, adorn the façade of the first early fourth-century relief, while Jupiter stands in heroic pose on the façade of the second fourth-century chariot in the British Museum. A fragmentary Augustan or early imperial terracotta plaque representing a similar vehicle also sports images of the Capitoline triad (Juno, Jupiter, and Minerva) on its façade, with Mercury, Hercules, and a Victory on the long side.[25] Such imagery suggests that these vehicles pertain to the gods in some manner—appropriate decoration for a *tensa*, a "vehicle of the gods."[26]

Apart from what appears to be Victory on the sides of the chariots minted under Augustus—a fitting figure for a triumph, of course, but also for a circus procession as Victory led the gods into the arena according to Ovid—the figural imagery on the numismatic *quadrigae* is unfortunately indistinct.[27] However, a bronze medallion minted under Antoninus Pius has a tall, boxy chariot with a pediment and no footboard, which sports the she-wolf suckling the twins in the Lupercal on the side and the legend ROM on the façade, indicating explicitly that vehicle belongs to Dea Roma, whose statue may sit on the apex of the pediment.[28] The chariots of deified Claudius and Vespasian were likewise explicitly glossed by their inscriptions, but on the observe, not on the chariots themselves. By contrast, the chariots minted under or in honor of Augustus were not so clearly labeled—though there seem to be oblique references to deified Julius Caesar and deified Augustus. In short, imagery and inscriptions strongly indicate that every one of these enigmatic, empty *quadrigae* belonged to the gods—whether traditional or imperial.

Even though the Augustan coins only tenuously identified the "owner" of the chariots as the deified Caesar, Julius Caesar was in fact honored with a *tensa* shortly before he was killed. According to Suetonius, "a *tensa* and a *ferculum* in the *pompa circensis*" figured among god-like honors that Julius Caesar received during his lifetime.[29] Cassius Dio, echoing Suetonius, maintained that in 45 B.C.E. the senate decreed "that an ivory statue of [Julius Caesar] and later that a whole car [a *tensa*] should appear in the procession at the games in the Circus,

Fig. 10. Empty quadriga *with lightning bolt,* denarius *of L. Rubrius Dossenus, 87 B.C.E., Rome (Harvard Art Museums/ Arthur M. Sackler Museum, Anonymous Gift, 1986.499; photography by Imaging Department © President and Fellows of Harvard College).*

along with the divine statues of the gods."[30] In other words, Julius Caesar was awarded a *tensa*, a sacred vehicle of the gods, to carry his *exuviae* (symbols or relics) and a *ferculum* (a litter) to carry his statue in the *pompa circensis*—honors that had previously been reserved for the traditional gods. The chariots minted under Augustus, then, may well represent the *tensa* of deified Caesar, upon whose legacy Octavian-Augustus certainly traded. Subsequent Julio-Claudian emperors likewise honored Augustus with a *tensa*, while Nero commemorated Claudius and Titus paid homage to Vespasian.[31]

Thus all the deified emperors from Caesar to Vespasian seem to have been honored with a *tensa* in the *pompa circensis*, at least if the identification of these enigmatic, empty chariots is correct. Indeed, many deceased members of the imperial house were honored in the circus procession: male members were typically granted an image on a *ferculum*, while female members were regularly gifted a statue borne in a *carpentum*, an honor attested both textually and numismatically.[32] After Julius Caesar, however, images of the deified emperor, as opposed to their *exuviae*, would no longer be carried on a litter. Rather, beginning with Augustus, statues of deified emperors would be borne on a *currus elephantorum*—a cart pulled by elephants, also attested in text and image—an honor eventually awarded to deified empresses and one whose numismatic representations would displace imperial *tensae* after Vespasian. Indeed, deified emperors and empresses would appear on elephant carts up to the short-lived Pertinax.[33]

The origins of this practice, the representation of a *tensa* as a synecdoche for the *pompa circensis* and the subsequent races, may lie in three coin-types minted by an otherwise unknown Lucius Rubrius Dossenus—an intractable bit of numismatic iconography. In 87 B.C.E., Dossenus minted a series of coins with Jupiter, Juno, or Minerva on the obverse and another enigmatic vehicle on the reverse (fig. 10).[34] Unlike other republican-era numismatic representations of "triumphal" chariots with low, swooping profiles, these vertically oriented, rectilinear chariots with mounting platforms, inverted and truncated triangular tops adorned with "acroterial" sculptures—Victory with a wreath or Victory driving a *biga*—and lateral decoration (a lightning bolt for Jupiter and an eagle clasping a lightning bolt for Juno and Minerva), stand well above the heads of their horse train.[35] In short, these chariots are tall and boxy with something like a pediment and imagery that suggests the divinity of the "owner." And so, *Coins of the Roman Republic in the British Museum* describes the vehicle as a "triumphal chariot … [which] recalls the solemn entry of [Jupiter's, Juno's, and Minerva's] chariots on the occurrence of the public games"—in other words, a triumphal (though ludic or circensian would be better) *tensa* in a *pompa circensis*.[36]

However, Michael Crawford, who characterized the chariot as a "triumphal quadriga," has strongly disputed the identification of these vehicles as *tensae*, noting the absence of a *puer patrimus et matrimus* and the lack of a motive to represent that processional vehicle.[37] But later numismatic examples of imperial "*tensae*," if that is what they are, also lack ritual attendants, while strikingly similar, indeed nearly identical, vehicles in other media do show attendants, very possibly a *puer patrimus et matrimus* along with *tensarii* and/or *nomenclatores tensarum*. Perhaps Dossenus wanted to be or had been an aedile charged with the organization of the public games, which prominently featured the *pompa circensis*— a goal or achievement that may explain these otherwise odd coin-types, following what Crawford himself calls "aedilician" types.[38] Signaling the *pompa circensis* by means of one of its most conspicuous features, *tensae*, which were almost exclusive to this procession, could certainly have been politically useful for someone like Dossenus. A similar motive, celebrating the Capitoline triad and the public games, may also explain the later Trajanic restoration of these same coins at least as well as any "triumphal" associations.[39]

Sabine Szidat similarly characterized Dossenus's chariots as "other parade chariots," since the odd, truncated triangular top does not conform to the pediment of standard imperial iconography, the key marker of a *tensa* as Szidat argues.[40] Following suit, Carsten Lange argues that the Rubrius coins depict a triumphal *quadriga* of the "slow" type due to the foot-board.[41] Even so, their rectilinear shape, pediment-like—or at least distinctive—top, scale (towering over the horse train), and ornament (lightning bolts and eagles) distinguish these obscure vehicles from more obviously "triumphal" *quadrigae* from the late republic. In short, the iconography suggests a processional vehicle connected to the gods depicted on the obverses. Additionally, the empty *quadriga* images minted under Augustus also have mounting platforms, but in every other respect those Augustan chariots resemble other imperial *tensae*. All things considered then, the distinctive shape and size (corresponding in most respects to what have been identified as imperial *tensae*) as well as the obverse imagery of the Rubrius coins intimate that these obscure vehicles may also have been *tensae*, sacred chariots that carried the symbols of the gods to the circus.[42] But, without explicit corroboration (a legend explicitly naming the type of vehicle, for example), the identification of these vehicles as *tensae* must remain tentative, though reasonable.

Conclusion

In the end, perhaps the magnificence of the triumph has blinkered the assessment of these coins and their imagery. Though the triumph was an immensely important and impressive ceremony, Rome witnessed a wide array of public spectacle and these other spectacles also constituted part of the construction and representation of political authority in both the republic and empire. In the republic, games were an essential weapon in the battle for honor and offices. As Cicero observed, "magnificent [games] are expected from the very best men in their year of aedileship"—an enormous expense, but one that could pay dividends in subsequent elections.[43] In 58 B.C.E., Marcus Aemilius Scaurus rather famously erected an impressive wooden theater, the memory of which benefitted his run for praetor in 56 B.C.E. and could have helped his, ultimately unsuccessful, campaign for consul in 54 B.C.E., as "the memory of his aedileship [was] not displeasing."[44] The republican competition for honors and offices may have abated during the empire, but emperors had their own uses for the *pompa circensis* and its related imagery. The *pompa circensis* was performed much more frequently than the triumph—perhaps as many as a dozen times per year during the high empire. More to the point, the addition of deified emperors and empresses allowed the circus procession to function like a surrogate funeral procession, from which deities, like deified Caesar and Augustus, were prohibited.[45] Representations of the *tensa*, which gesture to the procession and the games that followed, could thus signal both generous benefaction and, during the empire, dynastic claims—a very productive image indeed.

Notes

[1] *BMCRE* 1, 590.

[2] *RIC* 1² Augustus 259. See also, *OCRE* (*Online Coins of the Roman Empire*), http://numismatics.org/ocre/.

[3] *RIC* 1² Augustus 263.

[4] Lange (2016, 171–94) describes the back platform as a footboard.

[5] Szidat (1997, 31–37) identifies the pediment as the key iconographical marker of these vehicles.

[6] *RIC* 1² Augustus 108A (fig. 3); and *RIC* 1² Augustus 98, on which see Amandry 2013, 182.

[7] *RIC* 1² Augustus 223.

[8] Weinstock 1971, 57; and Rich 1998, 115.

[9] *RIC* 1² Augustus 119.

[10] See *OCRE RIC* 1² Augustus 108A; and *OCRE RIC* 1² Augustus 107A–113B, which construes tall, boxy and low, rounded chariots as the same type.

[11] *RIC* 1² Nero 4.

[12] *RIC* 1² Tiberius 60; and the corresponding entry in *OCRE*.

[13] *RIC* 2.1² Titus 360; a coin that the British Museum Collection Online description calls, parenthetically, a *tensa*: https://www.britishmuseum.org/collection/object/C_1864-1128-254.

[14] *RIC* 2.1² Vespasian 1127.

[15] *RIC* 1² Civil Wars 93; on which see Latham 2016, 114.

[16] Schäfer (2013, 321–23), with all the extant reliefs; and Lange 2016, 171–94.

[17] Musei Capitolini S 2464; on which see Alföldi 1973, 38; and Latham 2016, 115 and fig. 19.

[18] See Latham 2016, 215 and fig. 82.

[19] Ps.-Asc. *Verr.* 2.1.154; and see Latham (2016, 56–59 and 61–65) on *tensae*.

[20] Fest. 500L.

[21] Cic. *De har. resp.* 11.23; Plut. *Cor.* 25.3 (need to hold the reins); and Ps.-Asc. *Verr.* 2.1.154.

[22] Guidetti 2009.

[23] Accius, *Ex incertis fabulis* 39 (Non. 303L).

[24] *CIL* 6 740 = *ILS* 4216 = EDCS-17300881.

[25] Museo Nazionale Romano #4355; on which see Latham 2016, 57 and fig. 11.

[26] Diom. *Ars gramm.* 1 (Keil, *Gramm. Lat.* 1.376.10–11).

[27] Ov. *Am.* 3.2.45.

[28] Francesco Gnecchi, *I medaglioni romani, II: Bronzo, 1. Gran modulo* (Milan: Ulrico Hoepli, 1912), 22, nr. 117; on which see Toynbee 1944, 146 and fig. 41.3.

[29] Suet. *Iul.* 76.1; and Latham 2016, 108–12 with earlier literature.

[30] Dio Cass. 43.45.2.

[31] See Arena 2010, 53–102 on the *pompa circensis* in the early empire.

[32] E.g., Suet. *Calig.* 15.1; and *RIC* 1² Gaius 55l.

[33] E.g., Augustus's *currus elephantorum*: *RIC* 1² Tiberius 56 and Suet. *Claud.* 11.2; deified Marciana's elephant *biga*: *RIC* 2 Trajan 747 and 750; Pertinax: Dio Cass. 75.4.1 and Toynbee 1944, 102; and Latham 2016, 113–28 on imperial cult in the *pompa circensis*.

[34] Crawford 1974, no. 348.1–3 (fig. 10, no. 348.1). See also *CRRO (Coinage of the Roman Republic Online)*: http://numismatics. org/crro/.

[35] *Triumphator* in chariot, see, e.g., Crawford 1974, nos. 326.1, 358.1, 367.1–5, and 402.1a–b; and see Latham 2015, 202–5.

[36] *BMCRR* 1.311 n. 2.

[37] Crawford 1974, 362–63.

[38] Crawford 1974, 729. *BMCRR* (1.311, n. 1) suggests that Rubrius may have been a senator captured by Julius Caesar at Corfinum.

[39] *RIC* 2 Trajan 777–779; and Gallia (2012, 238–40), who considers them triumphal.

[40] Szidat 1997, 36–49.

[41] Lange 2016, 177.

[42] E.g., La Rocca 2007, 84 n. 42.

[43] Cic. *Off.* 2.57; and the insightful overview by Flower 2004.

[44] Cic. *Att.* 4.16.6 (89.6).

[45] Dio Cass. 47.19.2, 56.34.2, and 56.46.4.

References

Alföldi, A. 1973. *Die zwei Lorbeerbäume des Augustus*. Bonn: Habelt.

Amandry, M. 2013. "II.27 Denario di Augusto." In *Augusto*, edited by E. La Rocca, 182. Milan: Electa.

Arena, P. 2010. *Feste e rituali a Roma: Il principe incontra il popolo nel Circo Massimo*. Bari: Edipuglia.

Crawford, M. 1974. *Roman Republican Coinage*. 2 vols. New York: Cambridge University Press.

Flower, H.I. 2004. "Spectacle and Political Culture in the Roman Republic." In *The Cambridge Companion to the Roman Republic*, edited by H.I. Flower, 322–43. New York: Cambridge University Press.

Gallia, A. 2012. *Remembering the Roman Republic: Culture, Politics and History under the Principate*. New York: Cambridge University Press.

Guidetti, F. 2009. "*Tensam non tenuit*: Cicerone, Arnobio e il modo di condurre i carri sacri." *SCO* 55:233–48.

La Rocca, E. 2007. "I troni dei nuovi dei." In *Culto imperial: política y poder*, edited by T. Nogales and J. González, 76–104. Rome: L'Erma di Bretschneider.

Lange, C.H. 2016. *Triumphs in the Age of Civil War: The Late Republic and the Adaptability of Triumphal Tradition.* New York: Bloomsbury.

Latham, J.A. 2015. "Representing Ritual, Christianizing the *Pompa Circensis*: Imperial Spectacle at Rome in a Christianizing Empire." In *The Art of Empire: Christian Art in Its Imperial Context*, edited by L. Jefferson and R. Jensen, 197–224. Minneapolis, MN: Fortress Press.

———. 2016. *Performance, Memory, and Processions in Ancient Rome: The* Pompa Circensis *from the Late Republic to Late Antiquity.* New York: Cambridge University Press.

Rich, J.W. 1998. "Augustus' Parthian Honors, the Temple of Mars Ultor and the Arch in the Forum Romanum." *PBSR* 66:71–128.

Schäfer, T. 2013. "IX.5 Ciclo di rilievi Medinaceli." In *Augusto*, edited by E. La Rocca, 321–23. Milan: Electa.

Szidat, S. 1997. *Teile eines historischen Frieses in der Casa de Pilatos in Sevilla: Mit einem Exkurs zur Tensa.* Munich: Hieronymus.

Toynbee, J.M.C. 1944. *Roman Medallions.* New York: American Numismatic Society.

Weinstock, S. 1971. *Divus Julius.* Oxford: Clarendon Press.

Fashioning an Imperial *Aetas*: Nero's Portrait, the *Depositio Barbae*, and the *Iuvenalia*

Evan Jewell

Abstract

Zanker's (1987) seminal work on Augustus has led to burgeoning scholarship on the imperial image, which combines a variety of media to arrive at a more holistic understanding of imperial messaging strategies. Still, this approach has not yet been applied to the problem of the emperor Nero's young age at accession, nor to the history of Roman youth more generally. This paper therefore adopts a multimedia approach to the imperial image and its representation of age(ing) by reassessing one type in Nero's portrait series which appears to deliberately signal his physical maturity. This type, featuring an incipient beard, is dated to the period 59–64 C.E. on the basis of numismatic evidence. Tellingly, its inception coincides with Nero's Iuvenalia (or ludi Iuvenales), celebrated in 59 C.E. to mark his depositio barbae. By bringing Nero's portrait type into dialogue with the rite of the depositio and the Iuvenalia as an age-based spectacle, I frame this ensemble as an intensification of the advertisement of this rite by other male members in the imperial family, beginning with Octavian. I suggest that Nero's budding beard represents a carefully orchestrated instance of imperial self-fashioning that sought to mitigate the issue of Nero's youthfulness by deploying a physical and ritual sign of his maturing aetas.

The Youngest Emperor

When Nero became *princeps* at the unprecedented age of sixteen years and nine months, he and his advisors, together with the apparatus of the fledgling principate itself, were confronted with the problem of legitimating the rule of an adolescent who did not even qualify for the lowest rung on the *cursus honorum*.[1] For the later stylists of the youthful emperor, Tacitus, Suetonius, and Cassius Dio were fully cognizant of how Nero's young age offered them ample fodder for pinpointing one deleterious foundation of his principate. Hence at the beginning of Book 13 of his *Annales*, Tacitus frames Agrippina's perception of a hereditary rival to the principate, at the outset of Nero's reign, in the figure of Junius Silanus (also a descendant of Augustus), partially in terms of an age contrast—that is, between Nero "barely out of childhood" (*vixdum pueritiam egresso*) and Silanus's "settled age" (*aetate composita*).[2] So too, Cassius Dio ascribes Nero's extravagant banqueting to his youthful spirit; and while Suetonius dismisses "youthful mistake" (*iuvenili errore*) as a typical, if reasonable, explanation for such behavior—preferring to see it as a deep-seated character trait, in keeping with his biographical aims—he does tell us, in no uncertain terms, that the one honorific title Nero refused upon his accession, *pater patriae*, was due specifically to his age (*propter aetatem*).[3]

A year or so after the accession (55 or 56 C.E.), Seneca the Younger evidently recognized the problem of Nero's perceived youthfulness and sought to script the behavior of the young *princeps* in his *De Clementia* through the carefully crafted negative *exemplum* of Augustus's violent youth.[4] Also writing of *clementia* during this early period of Nero's reign, as Susanna Braund has suggested, Calpurnius Siculus alluded to Vergil's reference to the young Octavian in his first *Eclogue* as a *iuvenis* by deploying this very same age term to describe Nero.[5] In his fourth *Eclogue*, Calpurnius pushes this further: there Corydon wishes to win an august smile from the man who "rules the perpetual peace with youthful strength" (4.85: *perpetuamque regit iuvenili robore pacem*). Calpurnius's panegyric of Nero's youthfulness, like Seneca's, thus hinges on the assumption that Nero wanted to be perceived as a *iuvenis*.

To call the teenage Nero a *iuvenis*, rather than an *adulescens* or *puer*, may seem jarring, but the age terms applied to the *princeps* clearly had some political purchase. For the young Octavian had confronted a similar problem during his rise to power when labeled a *puer* by his elders and competitors, including Mark Antony and Cicero.[6] The insult was two-fold: the immaturity of the boy's aspirations and the penetrability implied by *puer*, if understood as connoting a servile body, thus had the potential to undermine the young Octavian's bid for political and martial power.[7] Such was the stigma attached to the term that Augustus seems to have had a *senatus consultum* passed prohibiting anyone (as a diminution of his *maiestas*) from using that age appellation to address or describe his person.[8] Besides legislation, clear changes in Augustus's

portraiture, especially marked with the introduction of classicism and idealism in his Prima Porta type, also allowed him
to signal to an audience that he had left behind the *pathos* of
his youthful years represented in the Actium-Alcudia type.[9]
Augustus's *aetas* was therefore tightly bound up with the
imperial messaging strategy famously reassembled by Paul
Zanker.[10]

A similar deployment of imperial messaging strategies has
been detected in Nero's later reign (after 64) with his cultiva-
tion of imagery associated with the sun and Hellenistic mon-
archy.[11] Yet in terms of his young age, previous scholarship has
passed over any serious investigation of the ways Nero and
his advisors might have sought to alleviate anxieties about his
youthfulness.[12] If we move beyond this early period of relative
stability, the year 59 and the constellation of messages ema-
nating from the emperor's facial hair offer us one opportunity
to recover an imperial messaging strategy designed to project
Nero's maturing age and thus allay any doubts about his legitimacy as *princeps*. This paper begins, then, with Nero's first
shave and the dedication of the shavings from his first beard
(*depositio barbae*) on the Capitol in 59. Situated as a coming-
of-age rite with a history of being advertised by male members of the imperial family, it was vaulted to unprecedented
importance by Nero's celebration of the *ludi Iuvenales*, or *Iuvenalia* and their age-based spectacles.

More tangibly, the second half of this paper turns to the
visual evidence attesting to Nero's beard as a visual sign of his
new maturity. Reexamination of both contemporary sculptural and numismatic imagery demonstrates that Nero's portrait of the Second Coiffure Type, which features an incipient beard and dates to the years 59–64, was an integral part
of the messaging strategy that revolved around the *depositio
barbae*. The bearded portrait type drew on precedents in portraiture from other male members of the imperial family and
could have harked back to the cognomen of Nero's patrilineal
branch of the *gens Domitia*, the Ahenobarbi. The historical
context of 59, however, argues for seeing the primary message
behind this portrait type as one intended to advertise Nero's
coming of age.

Nero's Coming of Age

Marking the end of the so-called *quinquennium Neronis*, the
year 59 was formative in the history of Nero's principate. The

death of Nero's mother, Agrippina, tends to overshadow the rest of the year's events, including the murder of another relative, Nero's paternal aunt, Domitia. Yet the latter episode provides the basis in Suetonius's account for Nero's decision to undertake the coming-of-age ritual of the first shave, the *depositio barbae*.[13] Stroking his beard, the aged and ailing Domitia told her nephew, who was visiting her bedside, that should he shave it off, she would die willingly.[14] With this impetus, the twenty-one or twenty-two year-old Nero proclaimed to his *proximi* that he would do so immediately and then ordered the doctors to kill her with an overdose so that he could inherit her property. But while Suetonius's anecdote frames Nero's *depositio barbae* as an act of caprice (*confestim*)—contributing to the overall biographical drive of the *vita*—the rest of our evidence, including Suetonius, points to the actual execution of this rite as a highly orchestrated act.

To turn to the ceremony itself, the rite appears to have occurred after the deaths of Agrippina and Domitia, and soon after the *Ludi Maximi*, such that we should not rule out the possibility that it was timed to coincide with the quinquennial anniversary of Nero's accession (October 13), or even his birthday (December 15).[15] Suetonius provides the only detail about the ceremony, separating the location of the shave itself from the *depositio*: Nero held the ritual shave during a gymnastic event in the Saepta, a space that had accrued a reputation for spectacles (especially gladiatorial *ludi*), accompanying the rite with the sacrifice of bulls; then we move to another space, the Capitolium, where he placed the beard in a golden *pyxis*, lined with pearls and dedicated it to Jupiter Capitolinus.[16] Connecting the two locations, we might imagine that some sort of *pompa* occurred. Immediately following the rite, Nero held *ludi* called the *Iuvenalia*, and Cassius Dio (via his epitomator Xiphilinus) is our only author to connect the spectacle directly to Nero's *depositio barbae*, telling us that the festival was "performed for his beard" (ἐτελέσθη ἐπὶ τῷ γενείῳ αὐτοῦ).[17] By all accounts then, the *Iuvenalia* appear to be a Neronian innovation, at least in name and emphasis.[18] Yet, before we assess their novel significance, we need to acknowledge that Nero's *depositio barbae* still drew on an established practice within the imperial family.

For the young Octavian had also celebrated his *depositio barbae* at the age of 24, in 39 B.C.E. when he was still susceptible to the *puer*-insult, as we have seen, and he could have used the occasion as one means of countering this discourse. Consequently, the ceremony was no small affair. As an example of the triumvirs' unprecedented spending measures, Cassius Dio relates how Octavian privately celebrated a festival to mark the rite, but also furnished another at public expense for the general public.[19] That Dio also describes Octavian's festival, like Nero's *Iuvenalia*, as an ἑορτή, the most proximate translation for the Latin *ludi*, points to some equivalence between the two celebrations, at least in Dio's reckoning, and strengthens the suggestion that Nero was partly drawing on the *exemplum* of Augustus's youth.[20] The young men who were marked out as Augustus's successors, save Tiberius, also all seem to have sported budding facial hair in their portraiture and an epigram by the Augustan era poet, Crinagoras of Mytilene, explicitly celebrated Marcellus's *depositio barbae*.[21] An Augustan paradigm was, therefore, already available for Nero's actions.[22]

Yet, in the meantime, innovations and exceptions had also occurred. Caligula had added a permanent day to the Saturnalia called *iuvenalis*, the precise character of which is opaque, though, as we will see, it may have also informed Nero's *Iuvenalia*.[23] But more significantly, we also know that Caligula's *depositio barbae* at the age of nineteen (after August 30, 31 C.E.) must have become part of the official articulation of his own life-course as a member of the imperial family, since Suetonius's account synchronizes it with his summons to Capri by Tiberius, marking the beginning of his ascent to the principate.[24] Importantly, Suetonius notes that Caligula's *depositio* was "without any of the public honor that had been connected to the coming of age of his brothers".[25] So while Caligula may not have had a festival or *congiarium* to mark the event, coming of age was clearly an advertised moment of imperial messaging in the lives of those males who might become *princeps*.

Nero's institution of the *Iuvenalia*, however, elevated the *depositio* and its message to a new level. We lack the evidence to compare it with the young Octavian's festival, but it seems that Nero's celebration was conceived as something new, especially as it featured, for the first time, the semi-private performance of the *princeps* himself. Yet, the one aspect of its novelty that concerns us here most was the age-based spectacle of its elite audience participants, who were enlisted as a component of the festival itself.[26] *Aetas* was no barrier to par-

ticipation, alongside *nobilitas* and *honores*, according to Tacitus.[27] Suetonius lays even greater emphasis upon age, briefly
summarizing the spectacle specifically in terms of the senior-
ity of its participants, that is, old men, consulars, old women
and matrons.[28] We must also envisage this spectacle happening amidst the applause of a conspicuous group of youths, a
claque dubbed the Augustiani.[29]

Cassius Dio (via his epitomator), who provides a more extensive treatment of the festival, singles out Aelia Catella as
his only named participant and "evidence" (τεκμήριον), despite noting the wide variety of participants in the spectacles.
For Aelia danced in a pantomime, and while known for her
family and wealth, Dio's account lays emphasis on the notable
fact that she was advancing in age as an octogenarian.[30] Dio's
focus on Aelia is the most telling indication that the spectacles of the *Iuvenalia* were received, at least in his sources,
as deliberately playing on age reversals. As John Starks has
adeptly noted in his study of actresses, "as an act in Nero's
Juvenalia [her performance] appears to have served as a spec-
tacularly degrading twist on the youthful energy of the pantomime… ."[31] The old becoming, or being forced to become,
young again, egged on by the young emperor and his youthful
Augustiani—could this be a Neronian extension of Caligula's
Saturnalian *dies iuvenalis*? Caligulan inspiration or not, the
literary sources suggest that the *Iuvenalia* had a particular
age-based thrust to its spectacles, suitable for the celebration
of a coming-of-age rite.

Visualizing Imperial Maturity: Nero's First Bearded Portrait

Though elaborate, and clearly memorable, to judge from Tacitus's repeated references to the senators' (non-)participation
in the festival, the *Iuvenalia* and the accentuation it brought to
Nero's coming of age were ultimately but a momentary pro-
jection of his imperial maturity.[32] A more enduring medium
was needed for this message and, as we will see, an imperial
portrait offered one well-established means to this end. Certainly Nero's position as a child in the imperial household had
occasioned the creation of an early series of puerile portraits,
sometimes attached to statues replete with the child's *bulla*
that date prior to 51 when Nero assumed the *toga virilis*. By
the time of his death, his final portrait type (64–68), distinctive for the *coma gradus formata*, marks the end of a process

Table 1. Nero's portraiture typologies

Date	Hiesinger 1975	Bergmann and Zanker 1981	Boschung 1993b	Other
pre-51 C.E.			Typus Parma	Mlasowsky 2001, "Velleia Typus"
51–54	Coin Type I			
54–59	**First** Coiffure Type; Coin Types II–III	Typus Cagliari (Typus II)	Typus Cagliari	
59–64	**Second** Coiffure Type; Coin Type IV	Typus Thermen-museum (Typus III)	Typus Thermen-museum	
64–68	**Third** Coiffure Type; Coin type V	Typus München (Typus IV)	Typus München-Worcester	

of increasing maturation witnessed in his preceding portrait types, as indicated by the corpulence of his neck, cheeks and underchin.[33] Thus while the lock scheme of the coiffure is the determining criterion for Nero's portrait typology, we witness, alongside this, clear physiognomic changes in the portraiture that track Nero's progression along the life-course.[34]

One such physiognomic change is the appearance of Nero's beard on his Second Coiffure Type (Coin Type IV) in Uwe Hiesinger's generally accepted typology (see table 1). This type is dated by its distinctive hairstyle, corresponding closely in profile view to that found in coin types from 59–64 C.E. (fig. 1), whereby a line of parallel locks running along the forehead shifts in the opposite direction after the juncture effected by a part in the hair, just above the right eye.[35] Uwe Hiesinger deemed one extant portrait, the so-called Terme portrait from Rome (fig. 2), the sole secure example of the type. Likely preserved in an imperial storeroom, the portrait's find spot on the Palatine Hill makes it an exceptional witness to the emperor's image within an imperial residence.[36] Nevertheless, Bergmann and Zanker have reasonably added three further examples of the type, but only one from Modena (fig. 3) shares the incipient beard of the Terme portrait. More recently, Naumann-Steckner has argued for another bearded marble example of the portrait type, now in the Römisch-Germanischen Museum at Köln.[38] The beards on each of these portraits are styled slightly differently, yet all are clearly incipient—as though the sculptors were keen to dis-

Fig. 1. Denarius, 60–61 C.E. RIC 1² 30. Münzkabinett, Staatliche Museen zu Berlin, inv. 18220695. Mint: Rome. Obverse: Nero, worn beard (?). NERO CAESAR AVG IMP. Reverse: Oak wreath. EX SC (center). PONTIF M[AX TR P] - VIII COS IIII P P (photographs by Dirk Sonnenwald, courtesy of Münzkabinett, Staatliche Museen zu Berlin).

play its potential for growth—and project an almost untamed vigor that is still carefully executed through the incised curls running from the ear lobe down to his underchin. The upper lip, philtrum, and upper chin display no trace of incision, betraying, perhaps, the control exercised over the growing beard even before the *depositio*.[39] It is notable, then, that the comma of hair, which protrudes before the ear, seems self-consciously placed to create the appearance of a more mature beard, blending at its termination, almost seamlessly, into the incised curls of the beard.

Unlike the more-developed beard of his third and final portrait type (64–68 C.E.), the *prima barba* of Nero's portraiture has garnered relatively little comment from portraiture specialists and historians alike, and it has never been explicitly connected to the *depositio barbae* itself. Uwe Hiesinger saw the introduction of the Second Coiffure Type as simply marking the quinquennial anniversary of Nero's reign.[40] In referring to the beard of this type, Hiesinger only claimed that there is a disjunction between the sculpted portrait type and the coin type, in that the latter is apparently always unbearded.[41] The disjunction, however, is a false one, since with the advent of high-quality photography and the increasing digitization of numismatic collections, we can now point to several examples of Hiesinger's Coin Type IV, which possess an incipient beard and allow us to make new observations.[42] The obverse of a denarius (fig. 4), minted in Rome and dating to 60–61 C.E. (*RIC* 1² 22), preserves the scraggly, incipient beard, which stands apart slightly more from the comma of hair in front of the ear than that seen in the sculpted portraits.[43] Again, aurei also from 60–61 and minted at Rome, reveal traces of the same incipient beard on Nero's portrait.[44] Yet, crucially, the beard is visibly present in all of these exam-

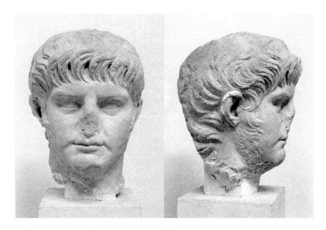

Fig. 2. Nero, marble portrait with incised beard. 59–64 C.E. Palatine Museum, Rome, ex Terme Museum, inv. 618 (photographs by Hartwig Koppermann, courtesy of DAI Rom: D-DAI-ROM-62.536, D-DAI-ROM-62.538).

Fig. 3. Nero, marble portrait with incised beard: modern copy of a no longer extant ancient portrait. 59–64 C.E. Museo Civico, Modena (photographs by Paul Zanker, courtesy of Fotothek München, Institut für Klassische Archäologie München: FM-PZ001008, FM-PZ001010).

ples. Comparison with other, more worn examples from the same series, suggests that the beard, positioned in the center of the coin face and therefore most susceptible to wear, could have been rubbed away with prolonged circulation (fig. 1).[45] The extra effort required by the detail of the intricate beard may have also meant that it was not always included in replacement dies.

How might we explain the advent of this first beard? We could point to Nero's ancestry and the cognomen *Ahenobarbus*—the family history of a beard with which Suetonius opens his *Vita Neronis* (1.1–2.2).[46] In this respect, Suetonius's anecdote, featuring his aunt Domitia stroking his beard, may well play on this familial connection. But as an explanation for the sudden appearance of Nero's beard—regardless of the date—the cognomen holds little weight; indeed, we might expect Suetonius to have made the role of his ancestry

25

Fig. 4. Denarius, 60–61 C.E. RIC 1² 22. Münzkabinett, Staatliche Museen zu Berlin, inv. 18220694. Mint: Rome. Obverse: Nero, lightly bearded. NERO.CAESAR.AUG IMP. Reverse: Virtus in martial dress, standing on a pile of arms, holding parazonium and spear. EX SC (center). PONTIF.MAX.TR.P.VII.COS. IIII.P.P (photographs by Dirk Sonnenwald, courtesy of Münzkabinett, Staatliche Museen zu Berlin).

in this event even more explicit when narrating the *depositio barbae*. If anything, Nero's bearded ancestry only accentuated the significance of the *depositio* all the more.

The timing of the first bearded portrait type, however, suggests a more event-specific impetus for the sudden emergence of the beard in Nero's image. One provincial numismatic example from Antioch and dated to 59–60 (*RPC* 1.4180; fig. 5), bearing the lock-scheme of Nero's First Coiffure Type (54–59, see table 1) created to mark his accession, may have precipitated the beard of the Second Coiffure Type and finds a striking sculptural parallel in a bearded portrait relief of Nero, also of the First Coiffure Type, from the Sebasteion at Aphrodisias (fig. 6).[47] Yet, it is significant that none of the coin series (including Hiesinger's Coin Type IV) from *imperial* mints at Rome, dating to 58–59, 59–60, or 62–63, as far as I have seen, display any traces (however faint) of a beard; only in 64–65 does the beard reappear in a rather more developed form with Nero's Third Coiffure Type (64–68, Coin Type V). The available numismatic iconography from the emissions of the imperial mint therefore suggests that Nero's first bearded portrait type at Rome could date to 60–61. While a full die study of the coin types in Nero's imperial coinage for 59–64 would allow greater confidence to be placed in this narrow chronological range, these initial findings suggest that the bearded version of the Second Coiffure Type was perhaps a portraiture development (*Weiterbildung*), designed specifically to commemorate Nero's *depositio barbae* in the year(s) immediately following the event. Certain cities in the eastern provinces, such as Antioch and Aphrodisias, may well have anticipated the advent of Nero's *depositio barbae* and thus slightly predate Rome in giving the *princeps* a beard, though one that does not resemble that disseminated from Rome.

Fig. 5. Tetradrachm, silver, 59–60 C.E. RPC 1 4180. Yale University Art Gallery, inv. 2001.87.4528. Mint: Antiochia ad Orontem. Obverse: Laureate head of Nero, bearded, with aegis. *ΝΕΡΩΝΟΣ ΚΑΙΣΑΡΟΣ ΣΕΒΑΣΤΟΥ.* Reverse: Eagle on thunderbolt, palm branch to the left. Ϛ = regnal year 6 (59–60 C.E.). HP = year 109 of the Ceasarian era (= 59–60 C.E.) (Yale University Art Gallery, public domain).

Fig. 6. Portrait of Nero with sculpted beard, First Coiffure Type (59–64 C.E.), from a marble relief featuring Nero wreathed by Agrippina minor. North Building, third story, Sebasteion, Aphrodisias, Turkey, inv. 82-250 (photograph by M.A. Dögenci, courtesy of the New York Excavations at Aphrodisias).

Fig. 7. Denarius, 38 B.C.E. RRC 534/3. Münzkabinett, Staatliche Museen zu Berlin, inv. 18210723. Mint: Moving with Octavian (Gaul). Obverse: Octavian, bearded. IMP CAESAR DIVI IVLI F. Reverse: M AGRIPPA COS / DESIG. (center of coin) (photographs by Reinhard Saczewski, courtesy of Münzkabinett, Staatliche Museen zu Berlin).

Again, Augustus's *exemplum*, as the young Octavian, may lurk behind the imperial image of the bearded youth, too. For in coin series from 43–36 B.C.E, Octavian's portrait also features a clearly incipient beard (fig. 7) and we may also possess a few portraits in marble and bronze of the bearded Octavian, known as Brendel's "Type B," though they are usually designated as portraits of his grandson and adopted son, Gaius Caesar (fig. 8).[48] While explanations of the bearded portrait have ranged from Octavian's mourning for Julius Caesar to his assimilation with Mars Ultor, the period in which the beard occurs also corresponds with the time of the *puer*-insult, when Octavian most needed to demonstrate that his ability could outrun his age.[49] Ability was at this time, to a large extent, military ability, such that it is also important to consider the potential for the beard to contain a degree of polysemy. For the presence of facial hair could also signal Octavian's military virility, manifest as the military stubble grown on campaign, and the majority of the coin series depicting him bearded come from the mints that moved with him while on campaign.[50] Hence, it is no coincidence that the bearded Octavian in the coinage disappears not with his *depositio barbae* in 39, but with his first major victory, over Sextus Pompey at Naulochus in 36, and the subsequent dissolution of the triumvirate in that year. The artifice of Octavian's bearded image is especially foregrounded by its continued appearance in the coinage after his *depositio barbae*, since Cassius Dio specifically tells us that after the ceremony he remained clean-shaven.[51]

The image of the beard was in Octavian's case, therefore, not tied to the absolute chronology of his first shave, but rather to the need to project the image of his maturity and military virility. That Crinagoras's epigram celebrating Marcellus's *depositio* tied it and his maturing into manhood directly to

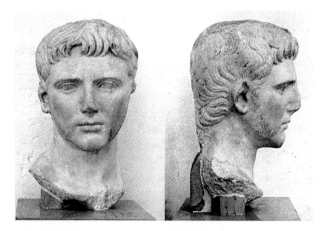

Fig. 8. Gaius Caesar, marble
portrait with incised beard.
Pollini (1987) Type V or
Brendel (1931) Type B. Arles,
Musée Lapidaire Païn, inv.
51.1.22 (photographs by Mrs.
G. Fittschen-Badura, courtesy
of Arachne, Archäologisches
Institut, Universität zu Köln:
Fitt70-26-05-766, Fitt70-26-
06-766)

Fig. 9. Germanicus, marble
portrait with sculpted side-
burns. From Medina Sidonia,
Baetica. Museo de Cádiz, inv.
7210 (photographs by Peter
Witte, courtesy of DAI Madrid:
D-DAI-MAD-WIT-R-16-79-01,
D-DAI-MAD-WIT-R-16-79-06).

his martial experience in Spain also speaks to this congru-
ence of attributes. And the same could be said for other male
members of the imperial household who followed suit, since
Gaius and Lucius Caesar, Drusus maior and minor, Germanicus, Nero Caesar, and Drusus Caesar all sport incipient
beards in some of their portrait types.[52] To take one example,
Brian Rose has proposed that the installation of portraits of
Germanicus (fig. 9) and Drusus minor at Medina Sidonia,
Baetica, can be chronologically tied to the time leading up to
their *depositio barbae* due to their visible sideburns.[53] Putting
aside the question of whether a beard can be taken as an accurate terminus ante quem, the beards on these portraits were
sculpted to form carefully groomed and prominent sideburns,
as though intended to draw the attention of viewers. Such
facial hair therefore deserves equal consideration as a visually
recognizable iconographic expression of a moment in the Ro-

man life-course, alongside the more acknowledged *bulla, toga praetexta* or *toga virilis.*

Nero's first bearded portrait type, like the rite of the *depositio barbae* itself, therefore followed an established precedent in the imperial family. Incised or sculpted in stone or metal, such a beard served a more long-lasting commemorative purpose than the rite itself or the *Iuvenalia*, reminding its audiences that the man before them was in fact now a man and no longer a boy. In this way, the year 59 was a fulcrum point in the history of Nero's reign and not just because it saw the demise of Agrippina or because it marked the end of the so-called "five golden years" of Nero's early principate. It heralded, quite literally, a new Neronian age.

Acknowledgements

I am grateful to Francesco de Angelis, Allison Kidd, Joe Sheppard and Jeremy Simmons for their suggestions and insightful critique of this paper at various stages, as well as feedback from audiences at Gothenburg, Sweden (ARACHNE VIII) and the 2018 AIA Annual Meeting in Boston. Assistance with obtaining images was kindly provided by Karsten Dahmen (Münzkabinett Berlin), Michael Kunst (DAI Madrid), Daria Lanzuolo (DAI Rom), Julia Lenaghan (Oxford), Clare Rowan (Warwick), Marko Runajić (Fotothek München), Lisa Schadow (Arachne, Köln), and Bert Smith (Oxford). Lisa Peck at the Columbia Media Center for Art History also provided invaluable technical advice.

Notes

[1] Cf. Griffin 2008, 116–17.

[2] Tac. *Ann.* 13.1.1: *verum Agrippina fratri eius L. Silano necem molita ultorem metuebat, crebra vulgi fama anteponendum esse vixdum pueritiam egresso Neroni et imperium per scelus adepto virum aetate composita insontem, nobilem et, quod tunc spectaretur, e Caesarum posteris.*

[3] Cass. Dio, 61.4.2; Suet. *Ner.* 26.1. On the refusal of *pater patriae*, see Suet. *Ner.* 8.1.

[4] Sen. *Clem.* 1.1.1–2, 1.9.1, 1.11.1–2. On the date of the *De Clementia*, see Griffin (1976, 407–11), and now Braund (2009, 16–17) who rightly reiterates the traditional reading that the work must date between Nero's eighteenth birthday (mentioned at 1.9.1: *duodeuicensimum egressus annum*) on December 15, 55 C.E. and his nineteenth birthday the following year. Henceforth, all dates are C.E. unless otherwise indicated.

[5] Calp. *Ecl.* 1.42–45 (esp. 44–45: *alma Themis posito iuvenemque*

beata sequuntur | saecula, maternis causam qui vicit Iulis), echoing Verg. *Ecl.* 1.42–45 (esp. 42–43: *hic illum vidi iuvenem, Meliboee, quotannis | bis senos cui nostra dies altaria fumant*). As noted in passing by Braund (2009, 13, n. 40), though she does not analyze the significance of the age term *iuvenis*. See also Martin 1996, 23–25. Although the date of Calpurnius Siculus has been highly contested, the majority of scholars, whom I follow, find him to be Neronian and writing during the early part of his reign (54–59 C.E.). For an exhaustive register of the scholarship on the question, see now Karakasis 2016, 1–2, nn. 1–2.

[6] For Octavian as *puer/pais*, sometimes *adulescens*, see Cic. *Phil.* 3.27, 4.3, 11.20, 13.24–25 (quoting Antony's letter to Hirtius and Octavian); *Att.* 14.12.2, 16.8.2, 16.11.6, 16.15.3, 11.14.1, 11.20.1; *Ad Brut.* 1.3.1, 1.18, 1.10.5, 1.16.5; App. *B. Civ.* 3.13, 3.18 (Antony calls him a *pais*), 3.19, 3.82; Cass. Dio, 46.41 (Octavian is specifically vexed at being called a boy by the senators in 43 B.C.E.), 50.17.3 (Antony's speech at Actium contrasts his and Octavian's age difference). McCarthy (1931) represents an early, if rudimentary, synthesis of this evidence.

[7] On the sexualization of the enslaved *puer*, see Williams 2010, 20–29.

[8] Servius, *Comm. in Verg. Ecl.* 1.42: *Iuvenem Caesarem dicit Octavianum Augustum: decreverat enim senatus nequis eum puerum diceret ne maiestas tanti imperii minueretur.* Although Servius's knowledge of the Augustan period has been faulted on some chronological points, in this case I see no reason to doubt this piece of content (as opposed to chronology), and all scholars appear to take it as sound evidence for a *consultum* at some point in Augustus's reign, for example see McCarthy 1931, 373; Malitz 2004, 407, n. 164; Schmitzer 2008, 165; Gardner 2013, 53.

[9] See Zanker 1973; Boschung 1993a.

[10] Zanker 1987.

[11] Bergmann 1998, 2013; Van Overmeire 2012. Cf. Cadario (2011, 180–88) who, also adopting a Zankerian approach, combines multiple readings of Nero's image, but does not consider the age-based reading I offer below.

[12] Although my argument builds on Griffin's (2013, 473) passing comment that: "Nero worked at turning his problems [as a youth] into an advantage, making, characteristically, a show out of it in the Juvenalia, games to celebrate his coming of age at 21."

[13] On the *depositio barbae* in general, see the previous treatments of Marquardt 1886, 599–600; Mau 1897, 33–4; Blümner 1911, 269–70; Eyben 1972, 693; Richlin 1993, 547; Obermayer 1998, 103–14; Harlow and Laurence 2002, 73; Williams 2010, 79–80; Laes and Strubbe 2014: 58; Toner 2015, 97–98; Degelmann 2017 and 2018.

[14] Suet. *Ner.* 34.5: *Quam cum ex duritie alvi cubantem visitaret, et illa tractans lanuginem eius, ut assolet, iam grandis natu per blanditias*

forte dixisset: "Simul hanc excepero, mori volo," conversus ad proximos confestim se positurum velut irridens ait, praecepitque medicis ut largius purgarent aegram; necdum defunctae bona invasit suppresso testamento, ne quid abscederet. See also Cass. Dio 61.17.1–2 and Jer. *Chron.* 2079G. Contrary to some translations, such as Rolfe's (1914) and Edwards's (2000), there is no indication in Suetonius's text of how fully grown Nero's beard was at this point; rather, as Kaster's (2016, 215–16) reading makes clear, *iam grandis natu* applies to Domitia's advanced age (nearing death), not to Nero's age or beard.

[15] I follow Champlin's (2003, 288–89, n. 62) relative chronology (after Cassius Dio's) for the year. Although no one has suggested a specific date for the *depositio barbae* or *Iuvenalia*, these two anniversaries seem to be the most likely opportunities for staging such an event.

[16] Suet. *Ner.* 12.4. Cass. Dio (61.19.1) provides Jupiter Capitolinus as the deity. Following Dio's chronology, Champlin (2003, 71–72, n. 62) has rectified Suetonius's incorrect placement of the *depositio* at the *Neronia* of 60, rather than at the *Iuvenalia*. Yet, it is unclear whether we should, following Champlin's rationale, no longer situate the *depositio* during a gymnastic contest at the Saepta simply because this is too "Greek" a spectacle for the "un-Greek" *Iuvenalia*. On the Saepta as a spectacle space, see *LTUR* s.v. Saepta Julia = Gatti 2000, 4:228–29; Bradley 1978, 88 and Kierdorf 1992, 177 with Suet. *Aug.* 43.1, *Calig.* 18.1, *Claud.* 21.4.

[17] Cass. Dio, 61.19.1. See also 61.21.1, where he reiterates this as the purpose of the festival in closing out his account of the year, though we should be wary of the epitomator's potential for repetition here.

[18] Bradley (1978, 81) notes the novelty of the festival. Harlow and Laurence (2002, 73) incorrectly read Ovid (*Trist.* 4.10.58: refers to his *carmina iuvenilia*) to posit that there was an earlier precedent for the *Iuvenalia*. Mourgues (1990, 197) suggests that the *Iuvenalia* may date back at least to the Tiberian period, since we have an inscription from Tusculum (*CIL* 14 2592) with a dedication by a certain *L(ucius) Priscus … curator lusus [iuvenalis]*, dated to 32–33 C.E. However, the text is doubtful and it is unclear how a *lusus iuvenalis* in Tusculum could correspond to *ludi Iuvenales* held by the *princeps* in Rome. For a reading that focuses on the ritual aspects of the rite and festival, see Degelmann 2018, 116–21.

[19] Cass. Dio, 48.34.3: ἀμέλει τὸν πώγωνα ὁ Καῖσαρ τότε πρῶτον ξυράμενος αὐτός τε μεγάλως ἑώρτασε καὶ τοῖς ἄλλοις ἅπασι δημοτελῆ ἑορτὴν παρέσχε.

[20] Cf. Champlin (2003, 272 n.53), who argues similarly for Dio's (61.17.2) translation (ἑορτὴν μεγίστην) of *Ludi Maximi*.

[21] *Ant. Pal.* 6.161: Ἑσπερίου Μάρκελλος ἀνερχόμενος πολέμοιο | σκυλοφόρος κραναῆς τέλσα πάρ᾽ Ἰταλίης, | ξανθὴν πρῶτον ἔκειρε γενειάδα· βούλετο πατρὶς | οὕτως, καὶ πέμψαι παῖδα καὶ ἄνδρα λαβεῖν. For attempts to identify Marcellus's bearded portrait,

see Balty 1977 and Andreae 1988. See also, Apollonides of Smyrna on a certain Gaius and Lucius's first shave at *Ant. Pal.* 10.19. See n. 52 below for the bearded portraits of male members of the Julio-Claudian family.

[22] Note that *imitatio Augusti* had explicitly characterized the first two years of Nero's reign. See Griffin 1984, 20–32; Champlin 2003, 139–40; and now, Hekster, Manders, and Slootjes 2014 and Hekster et al. 2015, who reexamine the numismatic evidence for claims to his Augustan lineage and find that it drops out of the iconography entirely after 56 C.E.

[23] Suet. *Calig.* 17.2: *Et ut laetitiam publicam in perpetuum quoque augeret, adiecit diem Saturnalibus appellavitque Iuvenalem.* Noted by Bradley 1978, 81; Ginestet 1991, 149.

[24] Cf. Willrich 1903, 100; Barrett 1989, 27.

[25] Suet. *Calig.* 10.1: *Transitque ad Antoniam aviam et undevicensimo aetatis anno accitus Capreas a Tiberio uno atque eodem die togam sumpsit barbamque posuit, sine ullo honore qualis contigerat tirocinio fratrum eius.* See Suet. *Tib.* 54.1 for the *congiarium* given to mark Nero Caesar's and Drusus Caesar's *dies tirocinii.*

[26] Cf. Gatti 1976–1977, 104–5; Bartsch 1994, 1–36, esp. 4–9.

[27] Tac. *Ann.* 14.15.1: *non nobilitas cuiquam, non aetas aut acti honores impedimento, quo minus Graeci Latinive histrionis artem exercerent usque ad gestus modosque haud viriles.*

[28] Suet. *Ner.* 11.1: *Iuvenalibus senes quoque consulares anusque matronas recepit ad lusum.*

[29] Tac. *Ann.* 14.15. Cf. Cass. Dio 61.20.4–5, Suet. *Ner.* 20.3 with Gatti 1976–1977, 103–21; Jaczynowska 1978, 270; Néraudau 1979, 371; Griffin 1984, 113; Mourgues 1988, 1990; Ginestet 1991, 9–10, 149–50; Bartsch 1994, 209, n. 15.

[30] Cass. Dio 61.19.2: τεκμήριον δέ, Αἰλία Κατέλλα τοῦτο μὲν γένει καὶ πλούτῳ προήκουσα, τοῦτο δὲ καὶ ἡλικίᾳ προφέρουσα (ὀγδοηκοντοῦτις γὰρ ἦν) ὠρχήσατο.

[31] Starks 2008, 114. Note, however, that he does not consider the wider age-based spectacle of the festival. Cf. Jory 1996, 8, n. 20 and Osgood 2017, 41.

[32] See Tac. *Hist.* 3.62, *Ann.* 15.33, 16.21.

[33] For the early pre-51 C.E. portraits and the problems of identifying these portraits with Nero, see Hiesinger 1975, 115–16 with nn. 13–14; Mlasowsky 2001, 107–10. For Nero's final portrait type from 64–68 C.E., see Hiesinger 1975, 120–22.

[34] Cf. Bergmann's 1982, 144 notion of *Zeittypen* as a conceptual explanation for the realism among imperial portraits at certain moments, including Nero's.

[35] Hiesinger 1975, 119; Boschung 1993b, 76, fig. 68 Zc.

[36] Hiesinger 1975, 119. On the exceptionality of its Palatine provenance, see Varner 2004, 68 with n.190; more generally on Nero's place in the history of the Palatine, see Tomei 2011.

[37] Bergmann and Zanker 1981, 324–27. Note, however, that the

portrait at Modena (Museo Civico) is a modern copy of a now-lost ancient sculpture. But such modern replicas have been shown to be fairly accurate, see Croisille 1999 and Varner 2004, 82 with earlier literature. See also Megow 1987, 214 A 99 pl. 35, 3 for a cameo with a light beard from Nancy, France, likely Second Coiffure Type, *pace* Bergmann 2013, 333. See Varner 2004, 65–66, 242 cat. 2.18, 256 cat. 2.65 for recarved portraits of Nero at Copenhagen and Yale, which appear to conform to this type and sported beards.

[38] Naumann-Steckner 2014; Boschung 2016, 84–85.

[39] Describing Nero's later Third Coiffure Type (64–68 C.E.), Cain (1993, 102) notes the control exercised over the beard there, too.

[40] Hiesinger 1975, 124, followed by Varner 2004, 49.

[41] Hiesinger 1975, 119: "Included is a light beard on the cheeks and underchin which appears here for the first time and is not reproduced on the coin portraits." Followers of Hiesinger: Bergmann and Zanker 1981, 322–26; Bergmann 1998: 148 ("Auf den Münzen ist er immer unbärtig."); Croisille 1999, 400–401; Schneider 2003, 65; Vout 2003, 455; Varner 2004, 48–49; Bergmann 2013, 336; Naumann-Steckner 2014; Boschung 2016: 84–85. Vout again (after Hiesinger) did not check the numismatic evidence, though she is aware of Nero's *depositio*. Cain (1993, 102 with n. 261) also dates Nero's beard to the late 60s while citing coins from *BMC*, but again did not look closely enough.

[42] I primarily used the OCRE (Online Coins of the Roman Empire: http://numismatics.org/ocre) database and its high resolution images to gather my numismatic data and assess the relevant coin types. Further research was conducted through the MANTIS database of the American Numismatic Society (http://numismatics.org/search/), as well as the online catalogues at the Münzkabinett in Berlin, the British Museum and Yale University Art Gallery.

[43] See also, for another example, *RIC* 1² 24, Münzkabinett, Staatliche Museen zu Berlin, inv. 18220688.

[44] See for example: *RIC* 1² 21, British Museum, inv. 1898,0803.16; *RIC* 1² 23, Münzkabinett, Staatliche Museen zu Berlin, inv. 18219758; *RIC* 1² 25, British Museum, inv. 1964, 1203.91.

[45] Griffin (1984, 22, n. 17) suggests, for the later bearded coin types (from 64–68), that wear may account for the absence of the beard in several examples.

[46] Griffin (1984, 20–22, esp. 22 with n. 17), only with respect to the beard of his final portrait type (64–68), points to the ancestral beard advertised by Cn. Domitius Ahenobarbus's denarii in 41 B.C.E. Cf. Vout 2003, 455.

[47] See Smith (2013, 74–78; cat. A 1), who is unaware of the contemporaneous coin type from Antioch, likely because, as *RPC* notes, a beard inconsistently appears on this coin type. It is important to note that in both the coin and relief portraits, Nero is laureate and the incipient beard, confined to the sideburns, is composed of round

tufts of hair, not elongated curls as in the Second Coiffure Type, the former being sculpted, the latter incised. A further bearded portrait in bronze, two fragments of which are now divided between the Musei Capitolini in Rome and the Walters Art Museum in Baltimore, originally found in Rome, may also represent another example of the First Coiffure Type, but with a beard that is more akin to the styling of those on the Second Coiffure Type. It may well then commemorate Nero's *depositio* and date after 59, *contra* Rose 1997, 115. See further Hill 1939, 407, Fittschen and Zanker 1985, 18–19, no. 18.

[48] Brendel 1931, 31–39. See the bearded examples identified as Gaius Caesar in Pollini 1987, cat. 19 (Florence), 21 (Erbach), 22 (Lugano), 23 (Modena), 25 (Berlin), 26 (Berlin), 28 (Rome), 29 (Aquileia), 30 (Arles), 31 (Verona).

[49] Mourning Julius Caesar: Brendel 1931, 38; Walker and Burnett 1981, 18. Vengeance for Julius Caesar: Walker 1991, 271. Assimilation to Mars Ultor: García Villalba 2016, 171–74. Pollini (1987, 71–75) argues that the beards of Gaius and Lucius Caesar do not represent the beard of mourning, but rather a military beard; however, he does not consider the *depositio barbae* as another (or complementary) explanation.

[50] *RRC* 517/1, 518/1, 523/1, 529/2, 534/2, 540/1. For (not entirely complete) catalogues, see Biedermann 2013, 32 and García Villalba 2016, 165–66; figs 1–2.

[51] Dio, 48.34.3: καὶ ὁ μὲν καὶ ἔπειτα ἐπελειοῦτο τὸ γένειον, ὥσπερ οἱ ἄλλοι. Noted by Vout 2003, 454. A disjunction also arises between the bearded examples of Nero's final portrait type (Third Coiffure Type, Coin Type V) and Dio's (63.9.1) report that while on tour in Greece from 66–67 he remained clean-shaven.

[52] See Rose 1997, 64 with nn. 85, 97, 132. Bearded portraits of Germanicus are collected in Fittschen 1987, but their connection to the *depositio barbae* remains to be assessed. For Drusus maior, see, for example, the sideburns on his portrait on the Ara Pacis procession frieze: Pollini 1987, 72–73. For a portrait of Drusus minor in Copenhagen, see Poulsen 1960, 20, 24. For Drusus (Germanici) Caesar's bearded portrait from Gabii, now in the Louvre, see Boschung 2002, 45; no. 6.3. For Nero (Germanici) Caesar's bearded portrait from La Spezia, see Boschung 2002, 92, no. 28.2, cf. Rose 1997, cat. 19) who identifies it as Germanicus. For Gaius Caesar, see n. 44 above, and Pollini 1987, 9, 35–38, 84–87, pl. 1.1 for incipient beards on the profile portraits (a combination of two different portrait types) of Gaius and Lucius Caesar on a sard intaglio now in Florence (Museo Archeologico, inv. 14914). This represents a sampling of a catalogue of over 35 bearded portraits of Julio-Claudian family members that I am currently preparing for publication.

[53] Rose 1997, 132, cat. 59: "Considering that Germanicus and Drusus have been presented as very young men here, the portraits were probably set up just before their *depositio barbae*."

References

Andreae, B. 1988. "Noch einmal zum Octavian Porträt Typus B." In *Ritratto Ufficiale e Ritratto Privato: Atti Della II Conferenza Internazionale Sul Ritratto Romano (Roma 1984)*, edited by N. Bonacasa and G. Rizza, 113–18. Rome: Consiglio nazionale delle ricerche.

Balty, J. Ch. 1977. "Notes d'iconographie Julio-claudienne IV: M. Claudius Marcellus et le type B de l' iconographie d'Auguste jeune." *Antike Kunst* 20:102–18.

Barrett, A. 1989. *Caligula: The Corruption of Power*. London: B.T. Batsford.

Bartsch, S. 1994. *Actors in the Audience: Theatricality and Doublespeak from Nero to Hadrian*. Cambridge, MA: Harvard University Press.

Bergmann, M. 1982. "Zeittypen im Kaiserporträt?" In *Römisches Porträt: Wege zur Erforschung eines gesellschaftlichen Phänomens*, 143–47. Berlin: Humboldt Universität.

———. 1998. *Die Strahlen der Herrscher: Theomorphes Herrscherbild und politische Symbolik im Hellenismus und in der römischen Kaiserzeit*. Mainz: Philipp von Zabern.

———. 2013. "Portraits of an Emperor: Nero, the Sun, and Roman *Otium*." In *A Companion to the Neronian Age*, edited by E. Buckley and M.T. Dinter, 332–62. Chichester: Wiley-Blackwell.

Bergmann, M., and P. Zanker. 1981. "'Damnatio memoriae'. Umgearbeitete Nero- und Domitiansporträts. Zur Ikonographie der flavischen Kaiser und des Nerva." *JdI* 96: 317–435.

Biedermann, D. 2013. "Zur Bärtigkeit römischer Porträts spätrepublikanischer Zeit." *Bonner Jahrbücher* 213, 27–50.

Blümner, H. 1911. *Die römischen Privataltertümer*. München: Beck.

Boschung, D. 1993a. *Die Bildnisse des Augustus*. Berlin: Gebrüder Mann.

———. 1993b. "Die Bildnistypen der iulisch-claudischen Kaiserfamilie." *JRA* 6: 39–79.

———. 2002. Gens Augusta: *Untersuchungen zu Aufstellung, Wirkung und Bedeutung der Statuengruppen des julisch-claudischen Kaiserhauses*. Mainz am Rhein: Philipp von Zabern.

———. 2016. "Nero im Porträt." In *Nero: Kaiser, Künstler und Tyrann*, edited by J. Merten, 82–88. Schriftenreihe des Rheinischen Landesmuseums Trier 40. Darmstadt: Konrad Theiss.

Bradley, K.R. 1978. *Suetonius' Life of Nero: An Historical Commentary*. Brussels: Latomus.

Braund, S. 2009. *Seneca. De clementia*. Oxford: Oxford University Press.

Brendel, O. 1931. *Ikonographie des Kaisers Augustus*. Nuremberg: Kreller.

Cadario, M. 2011. "Nerone e il 'potere delle immagini.'" In *Nerone*, edited by M.A. Tomei and R. Rossella, 176–89. Milan: Electa.

Cain, P. 1993. *Männerbildnisse neronisch-flavischer Zeit*. Munich: Tuduv.

Champlin, E. 2003. *Nero*. Cambridge, MA: Harvard University Press.

Croisille, J.P. 1999. "Néron dans la statuaire: le problème des identifications et des faux." In *Neronia V. Néron: histoire et légende*, edited by R. Martin and Y. Perrin, 397–408. Brussels: Latomus.

Degelmann, C. 2017. "Knaben, Männer, Bärte: Die römische barbatoria trennt Jungen von Erwachsenen." *AntW* 47:56–62.

———. 2018. "*Depositio barbae*. Das kaiserzeitliche Bartfest als Initiationsritus." *Theological Journal* 78:93–122.

Edwards, C. 2000. *Suetonius*. Lives of the Caesars. Oxford: Oxford University Press.

Eyben, E. 1972. "Antiquity's View of Puberty." *Latomus* 31:677–97.

Fittschen, K. 1987. "I ritratti di Germanico." In *Germanico: La persona, la personalità, il personaggio nel bimillenario dalla nascita*, edited by G. Bonamente and M.P. Segoloni, 205–18. Rome: G. Bretschneider.

Fittschen, K., and P. Zanker. 1985. *Katalog der Römischen Porträts in den Capitolinischen Museen und den anderen kommunalen Sammlungen der Stadt Rom*, Vol. 1. Mainz: Philipp von Zabern.

García Villalba, C. 2016. "La significación histórica del vello facial en los retratos de Octavio." *Anales de Arqueología Cordobesa* 27:161–82.

Gardner, H.H. 2013. *Gendering Time in Augustan Love Elegy*. Oxford: Oxford University Press.

Gatti, C. 1976–1977. "Studi neroniani II: gli Augustiani." *AttiCAntCl* 8:83–121.

Gatti, E. 2000. "Saepta Julia." In *Lexicon Topographicum Urbis Romae*. Vol. 4, edited by E.M. Steinby, 228–29. Rome: Quasar.

Ginestet, P. 1991. *Les organisations de la jeunesse dans l'Occident Romain*. Brussels: Latomus.

Griffin, M.T. 1976. *Seneca: A Philosopher in Politics*. Oxford: Oxford University Press.

———. 1984. *Nero: The End of a Dynasty*. New Haven: Yale University Press.

———. 2008. "Nero." In *Lives of the Caesars*, edited by A.A. Barrett, 107–30. Malden, MA: Blackwell.

———. 2013. "Nachwort: Nero from Zero to Hero." In *A Companion to the Neronian Age*, edited by E. Buckley and M.T. Dinter, 465–80. Chichester, UK: Wiley-Blackwell.

Harlow, M., and R. Laurence. 2002. *Growing Up and Growing Old in Ancient Rome: A Life Course Approach*. New York: Routledge.

Hekster, O., L. Claes, E. Manders, and D. Slootjes. 2015. "Nero's Ancestry and the Construction of Imperial Ideology in the Early Empire: A Methodological Case Study." *Journal of Ancient History and Archaeology* 1:7–27. DOI: 10.14795/j.v1i4.77

Hekster, O., E. Manders, and D. Slootjes. 2014. "Making History with Coins: Nero from a Numismatic Perspective." *The Journal of Interdisciplinary History* 45:25–37.

Hiesinger, U.W. 1975. "The Portraits of Nero." *AJA* 79:113–24.

Hill, D.K. 1939. "A Cache of Bronze Portraits of the Julio-Claudians." *AJA* 43, 401–9.

Jaczynowska, M. 1978. *Les associations de la jeunesse romaine sous le Haut-Empire*, translated by I. Wosczyk. Wroclaw: Zakład Narodowy imienia Ossolińskich.

Jory, E.J. 1996. "The Drama of the Dance: Prolegomena to an Iconography of Imperial Pantomime." In *Roman Theater and Society: E. Togo Salmon Papers*, edited by W.J. Slater, 1–28. Ann Arbor: University of Michigan Press.

Karakasis, E. 2016. *T. Calpurnius Siculus: A Pastoral Poet in Neronian Rome*. Berlin: Walter de Gruyter.

Kaster, R.A. 2016. *Studies on the Text of Suetonius' De Uita Caesarum*. Oxford: Oxford University Press.

Kierdorf, W. 1992. *Suetonius. Leben des Claudius and Nero: Textausgabe mit Einleitung, kritischem Apparat und Kommentar*. Paderborn: Schöningh.

Laes, C., and J. Strubbe. 2014. *Youth in the Roman Empire: The Young and the Restless Years?* New York: Cambridge University Press.

Malitz, J. 2004. "'O puer qui omnia nomini debes': Zur Biographie Octavians bis zum Antritt seines Erbes." *Gymnasium* 111:381–409.

Marquardt, J. 1886. *Das Privatleben der Römer*. Leipzig: S. Hirzel.

Martin, B. 1996. "Calpurnius Siculus' 'New' *Aurea Aetas*." *Acta Classica* 39:17–38.

Mau, A. 1897. "Bart." In *Real-Encyclopädie der classischen Alterthumswissenschaft*, edited by A. Pauly, 30–34. Stuttgart: J.B. Metzler.

McCarthy, J.H. 1931. "Octavianus Puer." *CP* 26:362–73.

Megow, W.-R. 1987. *Kameen von Augustus bis Alexander Severus*. Berlin: Walter de Gruyter.

Mlasowsky, A. 2001. Imago imperatoris: *Römische Kaiserbildnisse einer norddeutschen Sammlung*. Munich: Biering & Brinkmann.

Mourgues, J.-L. 1988. "Les augustians et l'expérience théâtrale néronienne." *RÉL* 66:156–81.

———. 1990. "Néron et les monarchies hellénistiques: le cas des Augustians." In *Neronia IV. Alejandro Magno, modelo de los emperadores romanos*, edited by J.M. Croisille, 196–210. Brussels: Latomus.

Naumann-Steckner, F. 2014. "Porträt des Kaisers Nero." In *40 Jahre Römisch-Germanisches Museum 1974–2014*, edited by M. Trier and F. Naumann-Steckner, 26–27. Cologne: Archäologische Gesellschaft Köln.

Néraudau, J.-P. 1979. *La jeunesse dans la littérature et les institutions de la Rome républicaine*. Paris: Belles Lettres.

Obermayer, H.P. 1998. *Martial und der Diskurs über Männliche "Homosexualität" in der Literatur der frühen Kaiserzeit*. Tübingen: Narr.

Osgood, J. 2017. "Nero and the Senate." In *The Cambridge Companion to the Age of Nero*, edited by S. Bartsch, K. Freudenburg, and C. Littlewood, 34–47. Cambridge: Cambridge University Press.

Pollini, J. 1987. *The Portraiture of Gaius and Lucius Caesar*. New York: Fordham University Press.

Poulsen, V. 1960. *Claudische Prinzen: Studien zur Ikonographie des ersten römischen Kaiserhauses*. Baden-Baden: B. Grimm.

Richlin, A. 1993. "Not before Homosexuality: The Materiality of the Cinaedus and the Roman Law against Love between Men." *Journal of the History of Sexuality* 3:523–73.

Rolfe, J.C. 1914. *Suetonius*. LCL. Cambridge MA: Harvard University Press.

Rose, C.B. 1997. *Dynastic Commemoration and Imperial Portraiture in the Julio-Claudian Period*. Cambridge: Cambridge University Press.

Schmitzer, U. 2008. "Wann kam Tityrus nach Rom? Ein Versuch der Annäherung an Vergils Eklogen." In *Vergil und das antike Epos: Festschrift Hans Jürgen Tschiedel*, edited by M. Strocka and R. von Haehling, 149–77. Stuttgart: Franz Steiner.

Schneider, R.M. 2003. "Gegenbilder im römischen Kaiserporträt: Die neuen Gesichter Neros und Vespasians." In *Das Porträt vor der Erfindung des Porträts*, edited by M. Büchsel and P. Schmidt, 59–76. Mainz: Philipp von Zabern.

Smith, R.R.R. 2013. *The Marble Reliefs from the Julio-Claudian Sebasteion*. Mainz: Philipp von Zabern.

Starks, J.H. 2008. "Pantomime Actresses in Latin Inscriptions." In *New Directions in Ancient Pantomime*, edited by E. Hall and R. Wyles, 110–45. Oxford: Oxford University Press.

Tomei, M.A. 2011. "Nerone sul Palatino." In *Nerone*, edited by M.A. Tomei and R. Rossella, 118–35. Milan: Electa.

Toner, J. 2015. "Barbers, Barbershops and Searching for Roman Popular Culture." *PBSR* 83:91–109.

Van Overmeire, S. 2012. "According to the Habit of Foreign Kings:

Nero, Ruler Ideology and the Hellenistic Monarchs." *Latomus* 71:753–79.

Varner, E.R. 2004. *Mutilation and Transformation: Damnatio Memoriae and Roman Imperial Portraiture.* Leiden: E. J. Brill.

Vout, C. 2003. "A Revision of Hadrian's Portraiture." In *The Representation and Perception of Roman Imperial Power,* edited by L. De Blois et al., 442–57. Amsterdam: J.C. Gieben.

Walker, S. 1991. "Bearded Men." *Journal of the History of Collections* 3:265–77.

Walker, S., and A. Burnett. 1981. *The image of Augustus.* London: British Museum.

Willrich, H. 1903. "Caligula." *Klio* 3:85–118, 288–317, 397–470.

Zanker, P. 1973. *Studien zu den Augustus-Porträts.* Göttingen: Vanderhoeck & Ruprecht.

———. 1987. *Augustus und die Macht der Bilder.* Munich: C. H. Beck.

Sabine Retrospective: Stylistic Archaism in Flavian Imperial Portraiture

Laura L. Garofalo

Abstract

Flavian imperial portraiture (69–96 C.E.), especially that of Vespasian, has long been compared with Republican veristic styles. Both are characterized by an emphasis on age and an apparent "warts-and-all" realism. However, in this paper, I argue for an additional, overlooked component of Vespasian's style: an appeal to the iconography and traditionalism of the Flavians' Sabine heritage. By the early imperial era, Sabine identity was associated with particularly lauded, rustic virtues. First, I review Suetonius and Tacitus's accounts of Vespasian's frugal habits, self-mocking sense of humor, and Sabine-inflected vowels. Next, I compare Vespasian's two portrait types to naturalistic private portraits from central and southern Italy, in order to demonstrate how Vespasian's public image may have evoked regional and nonelite iconography. In this way, Vespasian and his sons could appear both as dynasts looking to the ideals of the elite Republican past, as well as down-to-earth, Sabine men breaking from the Hellenizing excesses of the late Julio-Claudian dynasty.

Since the publication of Daltrop, Hausmann, and Wegner in 1966, Flavian imperial portraiture has been interpreted as an emulation of Republican veristic portraiture. In marked contrast with Nero's fleshy, Hellenizing portraits and the idealized, nearly ageless images of many Augustan and Julio-Claudian dynasts, portraits such as Vespasian's Copenhagen portrait have been thought to evoke the stylized, supposedly "warts and all" image of verism, an extremely realistic-seeming portraiture style of the late Republic (second and first centuries B.C.E.). In turn, the veristic style and its Flavian emulation have been thought to appeal to an elite iconography of age, experience, and accordant *gravitas*—a conservative image through which Vespasian may have sought to stabilize his new dynasty after the upheaval of civil war in 68/69 C.E. Scholars have also looked to Vespasian's more advanced age at accession—around 60 years old—and to the conservatism of his reign for other, biographical factors that may have informed the new dynastic image. A look to the past, and particularly the Augustan past, is generally accepted as a primary source of inspiration for the beginning of the new dynasty, as seen in Flavian coins evoking peace and restoration of order.[1]

However, I would suggest another influence that shaped the dynasty's new image—the Flavians's Sabine heritage. Drawing upon their family origins in the Apennine mountains, Vespasian and his sons evoked the legendary history of the Sabine *gens* and contemporary cultural associations with Italian hill-country. In this paper, I argue that a rustic, Sabine persona was one element of Vespasian's public image, as demonstrated in historical sources as well as in portraiture. In Tacitus, Suetonius, and Dio Cassius's accounts, Vespasian's Sabine identity comes to the fore in a series of telling details concerning his habits and down-to-earth persona. In portraiture, this image is conveyed through a naturalistic portrait style—a less-extreme, yet still seemingly "realistic" style that developed alongside idealized Julio-Claudian court styles. This naturalistic style is seen particularly in regional and nonelite portraiture, as well as in Vespasian's portraiture. In each case, Vespasian's public image subverts the usual norms of elite ideology and iconography in favor of an intentionally humbler image.

As Emma Dench and Gary Farney have demonstrated, the Apennine region of Italy was associated with cultural memories of the Roman past, such as the rape of the Sabine women, incorporation into early Rome, and legendary Sabine kings of Rome, such as Numa.[2] While luxury and excess were part of the Sabine image during the mid-Republic, by the late first century B.C.E., old-fashioned habits and attitudes dominated Roman perceptions of Sabine identity.[3] As Wiseman and Farney have illustrated, several late Republican families seem to have used the cognomen "Sabinus" as a shorthand for traditionalism and old-time virtue.[4] Cicero and Livy also allude to the frugality and traditionalism of the Sabine region and its inhabitants,[5] while, according to Servius, the elder Cato is said to have sought out origins for the region's characteristic austerity in a supposed Spartan forefather of the Sabines, Sabus the Lacedaemonian.[6]

These hints of local Sabine character and its rustic associations emerge in several ancient sources describing Vespasian
and his sons. Suetonius sets Vespasian's origins in a relatively
undistinguished family line, citing roles for his father as a tax-
collector and mentioning a nickname for Vespasian regarding
mid-career mule-driving.[7] Suetonius also discusses the Flavian family's origins near Sabine Reate, as well as Vespasian's
favor for and frequent returns to his grandmother's farm at
Cosa, further north.[8] Later, upon his accession, Vespasian
was well known for his supposed frugality and even stingi-
ness, recounted in several stories—including an actor mim-
ing Vespasian at his funeral, who, when told how much the
funeral would cost, joked that they should use a tenth of the
cost and throw him (the emperor) into the Tiber.[9] When
some in the court attempted to link the family origins in
Reate to a legendary companion of Hercules, Vespasian supposedly laughed them away, according to Suetonius:

> Ceteris in rebus statim ab initio principatus
> usque ad exitum civilis et clemens, mediocrita-
> tem pristinam neque dissimulavit umquam ac
> frequenter etiam prae se tulit. Quin et conantis
> quosdam originem Flavii generis ad conditores
> Reatinos comitemque Herculis, cuius monumen-
> tum exstat Salaria via, referre irrisit ultro.

> In other matters [Vespasian] was unassuming
> and lenient from the very beginning of his reign
> until its end, never trying to conceal his formerly
> lowly condition, but often even parading it. In-
> deed, when certain men tried to trace the origin
> of the Flavian family to the founders of Reate and
> a companion of Hercules whose tomb still stands
> on the Via Salaria, he laughed at them for their
> pains... (Suet. *Vesp.* 12)[10]

Vespasian's refusal of a mythological heritage aligns well with
a public image of humble origins, even one tied to local cults
in his hometown, Reate. The emperor also famously joked
about becoming a god on his deathbed, in a similar subver-
sion of imperial honors.[11]

Other anecdotes, concerning Vespasian's stubborn, rustic
vowel pronunciation and his modest manners (including an
unclassed, unguarded *salutatio* held in the Gardens of Sal-
lust), suggest a similar public image of humility and approach-

ability.[12] These characterizations are echoed by Tacitus, who highlights a return to more modest values through the rise of Italian elites, explicitly pointing to Vespasian's frugality and simpler lifestyle as a key example of this trend:

> …luxusque mensae a fine Actiaci belli ad ea arma, quis Servius Galba rerum adeptus est, per annos centum perfusis sumptibus exerciti paulatim exolevere…

> postquam caedibus saevitum et magnitudo famae exitio erat, ceteri ad sapientiora convertere. Simul novi homines, e municipiis et coloniis atque etiam provinciis in senatum crebro adsumpti, domesticam parsimoniam intulerunt, et quamquam fortuna vel industria plerique pecuniosam ad senectam pervenirent, mansit tamen prior animus. Sed praecipuus adstricti moris auctor Vespasianus fuit, antiquo ipse cultu victuque, obsequium inde in principem et aemulandi amor validior quam poena ex legibus et metus…

> Luxury and sumptuous dining were practiced for one hundred years with profligate indulgence from the Battle of Actium down to the civil war which put Servius Galba in charge of the state. This gradually began to fall out of fashion…

> Following the savage persecutions and the disaster attended by fame, the survivors turned to wiser actions. At once, new men from the municipia and colonies—and even from the provinces—steadily entered the Senate and brought with them innate austerity. Although most had come to a wealthy old age through fortune or industry, yet they still retained their old mind-set. But the most conspicuous promoter of these *mores* was Vespasian, himself of old-fashioned habit and manner. At that point, obedience to the emperor and a desire to emulate him was stronger than punishment of the law and fear.[13] (Tac. *Ann.* 3.55.1, 3–4)

These stories, though relating seemingly minor details, emphasize Vespasian's humble origins, or even insist upon them, creating an image of a simple, frugal man of Sabine descent—perhaps even a Marian-style new man.[14] It seems less of a co-

Fig. 1. Portrait of Vespasian, Ny Carlsberg Glyptotek, Copenhagen, inv. 2585 (photograph by O. Haupt, courtesy of the Ny Carlsberg Glyptotek).

incidence that these ideals and anecdotes align well with the first-century C.E. image of the Apennine tribes and Sabine *gens*, both cultivated and imagined. If this was indeed part of Vespasian's new public image, as a plain-speaking general with deep Italian roots, it should not be surprising that this ideal finds its way into public images of the dynasty.

In terms of iconography, portrait types of the Flavian dynasts are often complicated by recutting, due to the frequent reuse of portraits of Nero. In the case of Domitian, many portraits were recut a second or third time after his death.[15] However, for Vespasian, the general consensus is for two major types—the first and primary type, most often exemplified by the Copenhagen portrait (fig. 1),[16] depicts a lined, severe, and usually balding figure; a second, more idealized portrait type can be found in the Lucus Feroniae portrait (fig. 2).[17] The second type features slightly softer, less intensely fur-

Fig. 2. Portrait of Vespasian, Museo Archeologico di Lucus Feroniae, Capena (photograph by J. Felbermeyer, D-DAI-ROM-62.517).

rowed features, thought to represent a more idealized pre-accession portrait or a posthumous, divinized image. Yet, according to Varner's count, 10 out of 16 portraits of Nero recut into Vespasian are categorized as Vespasian's second portrait type (including the Lucus Feroniae portrait itself), perhaps explaining its more classicizing, less severe depiction of age—and fuller heads of hair.[18] In both of Vespasian's portrait types, however, the emperor is depicted with several details of age, from a furrowed brow, deep naso-labial creases, and crow's feet around the eyes, to a lined neck and slightly sagging cheeks. In a few instances of portraits recut from busts of Nero, as Varner notes, these details are especially

heavy handed, suggesting that age and experience were an essential marker of Vespasian's image, in explicit contrast with
the more youthful, fleshy styles of Neronian portrait types.[19]

While Vespasian's iconographic emphasis on age and se-
verity are reminiscent of the elite iconography of Republican
verism, I suggest that these details also evoke early imperial iconographic changes beyond verism. Verism, an elite,
Republican-era style characterized by intense, or even exaggerated markers of advanced age, had its particular heyday in
the second and first centuries B.C.E.[20] A less-extreme strand
of realism, which I will call early imperial naturalism, existed
alongside verism and persisted into at least the first century
C.E. Since this type of naturalism often is found in nonelite
group funerary monuments, this style has been read as an
emulation of Republican verism, suggesting a less intense, or
even banal form of "trickle-down" style. However, naturalism
developed its own stylistic qualities and connotations.[21]

First, early imperial naturalism often combined its appeal to realism with varying degrees of Augustan and Julio-
Claudian styles, especially in funerary reliefs. One example
of stylistic interplay between naturalism and early imperial
styles can be found in a monument now in Centrale Montemartini (fig. 3).[22] The portraits in this relief, dated to the
late first century B.C.E., combine Augustan-era hairstyles
with varied signs of aging, such as lined faces and deep naso-
labial creases. For example, the male figure on the far right
(fig. 4) combines a version of an Augustan-inspired coiffure
with an intensely lined brow, pronounced crow's feet, and sagging, slightly sunken cheeks. Many of these same, carefully
modulated details of age characterize portraits of Vespasian
several decades later.

Similar naturalistic styles continued in private portraiture through the first century C.E., alongside and often in

*Fig. 3. Funerary Relief, Cen-
trale Montemartini, Musei
Capitolini, Rome, inv. 2231
(photography by K. Anger,
D-DAI-ROM-2001.2106).*

Fig. 4. Detail of Centrale Montemartini funerary relief (photograph by G. Fittschen-Badura, https://arachne. dainst.org/entity/2235956).

dialogue with imperial court styles.[23] Though many of these portraits have been identified as "nonelite," and therefore have been presumed to emulate elite styles (such as Republican verism), this humbler, hybrid form of naturalism was much more contemporary and likely more widespread by 69 C.E., when Vespasian rose to power. Rather than assuming that the Flavians looked to nearly century-old elite veristic styles of the late Republic, Vespasian's image of age and experience was likely informed by and understood as part of a tradition of nonelite and Italian provincial iconography—both humbler (or vaunted as such) and more conservative.

Portraits with a secure find spot in Sabine territory are difficult to identify, due in part to the collection history of Roman portraits.[24] Many museum catalogues list only previous collectors or rough areas of origin; to complicate this, the proximity of Rome as a major antiquities market likely drew many portraits found in the Apennines. However, a few portraits now in the Museo Archeologico Nazionale, Chieti provide some suggestive parallels. For example, one well-known first-century B.C.E. portrait of a man (fig. 5), found

Fig. 5. Portrait of a man, Museo Archeologico Nazionale, Chieti, inv. 4430 (photograph by G. Singer, D-DAI-ROM-67.845).

in Foruli, a Roman-era Sabine town near modern Scoppito, Italy, shares several features with the Copenhagen portrait of Vespasian.[25] Note in particular the small, slightly recessed eyes, lined brow and nose bridge, crows-feet around the eyes, and deeply incised naso-labial creases. Several other mid- to late first-century B.C.E. portraits from Alba Fucens, another Sabine town, and Teate, a precursor to modern Chieti, suggest similar features of advanced age.[26] For example, a mid-first-century B.C.E. portrait found in Teate (fig. 6) depicts a man with a deeply furrowed brow, lined neck, and sunken cheeks.[27] The small, recessed eyes, thin, nearly lipless mouth, and slight turn of the head also recall the Copenhagen portrait of Vespasian (fig. 1), albeit with a more elongated face and fuller head of hair.

A few regional portraits from Samnium, a similarly mountainous region further south from Sabine territory, also reflect this style.[28] For example, a portrait of a middle-aged looking man (fig. 7), now in the Ny Carlsberg Glyptothek, shares similar features.[29] This portrait, said to come from Anfidena in Samnium,[30] includes heavy facial creases, a rounded and dimpled chin, and small, slightly recessed eyes, again much like the Foruli man (fig. 5) and the Copenhagen portrait of Vespasian (fig. 1). Similar features can be found in

Fig. 6. Portrait of a man, Museo Archeologico Nazionale, Chieti, inv. 8603 (D-DAI-ROM-8254).

funerary relief portraits further south in Samnium, including a Claudian-era limestone relief of a man and woman now in the Museo del Sannio in Benevento (fig. 8).[31] Here again, a balding male figure is portrayed with small eyes, a cleft chin, prominent naso-labial creases, and wrinkled cheeks, continuing in a similar naturalistic style.

When considered alongside ancient sources' emphasis on Vespasian's supposed humility and stubborn Italian provincial origins, the emperor's naturalistic portrait style reflects shared, perhaps regional iconographic norms. As seen in the private portraits discussed above (fig. 5–8), similar details appear, including blocky heads with small eyes, lined brows, furrowed cheeks, and thin-lipped mouths. Though it may be impossible to identify a particular "Sabine" style, the similarity between Vespasian's portraiture and these regional, naturalistic portraits is suggestive.[32] Vespasian's public image as a frugal Sabine, outlined above, as well as the cultural ideals

Fig. 7. Portrait of a man, Ny Carlsberg Glyptotek, Copenhagen, inv. 2116 (Johansen 1994, 81).

that followed from popular characterizations of his "earthy" Sabine identity, would make a canny choice for a new dynastic image, especially for a man who sought to separate himself from the ideals and imagery of the Julio-Claudians.[33]

Further, I would suggest that Vespasian's appeal to the past, and particularly the cultural associations of his Sabine heritage, drew not only from the ideals of the Italian countryside, but also from nonelite portraiture. Rather than appealing directly to the elite ideals of the Republic, it is possible that Vespasian sought to look like a rustic military man and in doing so, looked to more recent, naturalistic portraiture from Italy. In this way, we could see an imperial portraiture style inspired by, as much as inspiring, private portraiture, forming a more multivalent model of influence and reimagination than "trickle-down style" and the *Zeitgesicht* might usually assume.

Fig. 8. Funerary relief, Museo del Sannio, Benevento, inv. 634 (photograph by H. Singer, D-DAI-ROM-68.311).

When combined with a humble public image, the same details of age that link Vespasian's portraiture to elite Republican verism then might also be read as assimilations to a humbler ideal of early imperial naturalism, seen in the realistic-seeming details of age in Italian private portraiture. Seen from this angle, this strand of nonelite naturalism allows Vespasian to present himself in a trustworthy, down-to-earth guise, familiar to a wider swath of humbler Romans, or even as a proud, *novus homo* to the purple. In contrast with Galba's palace *stemmata* and Vitellius's vaunted mythological ancestors, Vespasian's embrace of modesty was an unusual, if, perhaps, calculated stance.[34] It seems reasonable to look to other, more contemporary sources of influence, including regional portraiture, rather than solely seeking a link to the fading Republican past.

In sum, I have argued that Flavian imperial portraiture is more multivalent and draws from more diverse visual sources than is usually assumed. The iconographic naturalism, or supposed realism of Vespasian's portraits likely engaged with both elite and nonelite imagery, evoking the traditionalism and austerity implied by the Flavians' Sabine heritage as well as the deeper past of Republican verism. In this way, Vespasian and his sons could appear in either or both visages—as dynasts looking to the ideals of the Republican past, as well as down-to-earth, Sabine new men breaking from the excesses of the more recent, Julio-Claudian past.

Notes

I am grateful to Dustin Dixon, Jessica Lamont, audience members in Boston and to the three anonymous reviewers for their comments and suggestions on this chapter. I would also like to thank the image permissions staff at the Ny Carlsberg Glyptotek, the Digital Archaeology Lab at the University of Cologne, and at the DAI Rome, especially Daria Lanzuolo. Any errors that remain are my own.

[1] On Flavian emulation of Augustan symbols and policies, see Rosso 2009a; Hurlet 2016, 30–33; and Tuck 2016, 109–10. On Flavian antiquarianism, see Gallia 2012 and Cox 2014.

[2] On Sabine and Appenine culture more broadly, see Dench 1995; Farney 2007, 78–124; 2011; and Farney and Masci 2018. See also Farrell 2014 on associations between the Roman countryside and an older, more virtuous past.

[3] Dench 1995, 85–94 and Farney 2007, 97–101.

[4] For example, Cic. *Fam.* 15.20.1; see also Wiseman 1971, 257–58 and Farney 2007, 90–97 and 215.

[5] For example, see Livy 1.18.4 on Numa's austere Sabine character and Cic. *Lig.* 32 on Sabines as *fortissimi* and Sabine land as *robur rei publicae*. Farney (2011) examines how these ideals later came to embody a broader Italian identity.

[6] Serv. *Ad Verg. Aen.* 8.637–638 = Cato *Orig.* frg. 51 (*FRHist* 5.51), with Dench 1995, 85–87 and Farney 2007, 101–4.

[7] Suet. *Vesp.* 1–2 and 4.

[8] Suet. *Vesp.* 2.

[9] Suet. *Vesp.* 19.2. On Vespasian's frugality, see Suet. *Vesp.* 16, 23 and Dio 65.10–11. On frugality in Roman-era Sabines, see Farney (2007, 112–15).

[10] Translation adapted from Rolfe 1998.

[11] Suet. *Vesp.* 12; 23.4 with Levick 2005, 74. On laughter as part of Vespasian's public image, see Suet. *Vesp.* 22–23 and Dio Cassius 65.11, with Beard 2014, 130, 133–34.

[12] Rustic vowels: Suet. *Vesp.* 22. See also Cic. *De or.* 3.42–46, with Dench 1995, 94, n. 128 and Farney 2007, 123, for Cicero complaining about politicians adopting a rustic accent. On the *salutatio*: Dio Cass. 65.10.4; Suet. *Vesp.* 12.

[13] Cf. Tac. *Hist.* 2.5.1, Farney (2011, 226–27) and Woodman and Martin 1996, 401, 406 with similar references. Translation adapted from Farney 2011.

[14] On Vespasian's career, see Levick 2005. Dench (2005, 182–87) discusses regional identity and Cicero's conception of austere Italian nobles with old-fashioned virtue. See especially Dench 2005, 185–86 and Wiseman 1971, 107–11 on the complexity and possible retrojection of "new man" ideology.

[15] See Bergmann and Zanker 1981 and Varner 2004, 52–61 and 111–35, for overviews with earlier bibliography, as well as Wood 2016.

[16] Ny Carlsberg Glyptotek, Copenhagen, inv. 2585. Marble, 0.4 m. ca. 70 C.E. See Johansen 1995, 28–29, no. 3 and Rosso 2009b for earlier bibliography.

[17] Museo Archeologico di *Lucus Feroniae*, Capena. Marble, 0.34 m. Third quarter of the first century C.E. Found in Lucus Feroniae in 1953. See La Rocca, Parisi Presicce, and Lo Monaco 2011: 266, cat. 4.13 (P. Aureli and G. Colugnati) and Varner 2004: 52–53, cat. 2.22, fig. 46a–d, with earlier bibliography.

[18] Varner 2004, 52–55 following Bergmann and Zanker 1981.

[19] Varner 2004, 54–55.

[20] See Rose 2008, 102–18 for an overview of scholarship on veristic portraiture, with earlier references. See also Pollini 2007, 253–55 on the history of the modern term "verism."

[21] Though verism and naturalism both appear to convey "realism" in the sense of suggesting fidelity to the appearance of a subject, both were culturally and ideologically charged and could convey group identity as much as individualism. See, for example, Gruen 1992, 152–82 on Roman cultural identity and the veristic style as well as Clarke 2003; Petersen 2006; and de Angelis et al. 2012 on "freedman art" in the history of scholarship on Roman art. On "naturalism" as an alternative term to "realism" in Hellenistic portraiture, see von den Hoff 2007.

[22] Centrale Montemartini, Musei Capitolini, Rome, inv. 2231. Marble, 0.58 x 2.30 x 0.40 m. Late first century B.C.E., found near the Porta Flaminia in 1889. See Kockel 1993, cat. no. F1, pp. 119–20, Taf. 31a, 32a–d, 33a and b for discussion and further bibliography.

[23] Comparisons with imperial court styles often complicate or prejudice stylistic dates. For example, see the inscribed portrait bust of L. Licinius Nepos (Getty Villa, Malibu, inv. 85.AA.111), previously identified as Trajanic on the basis of style, now redated to the first quarter of the first century C.E. Panciera and Zanker (1988–1989) presented a new reading of the inscription (*CIL* 6 9659), the funerary context, and a reevaluation of the portrait style, which Zanker connects to "freedmen" portraits of the late Republic to early Augustan era. The authors, however, surprised by the high quality of the portrait, suggest an elite patron (1988–1989: 383–84).

[24] On imprecision in describing archaeological provenance, see Marlowe (2013, 44–52). Marlowe (2013, 81–98) also discusses the problematic, often circular logic of class and style in Roman portraiture.

[25] Museo Archeologico Nazionale, Chieti, inv. 4430. Marble, 0.27 m. mid-first century B.C.E., from Foruli. Di Mino and Nista 1993, cat. no. 9, pp. 52–53 and Tav. XI. Zanker (1976, 604, fig. 19) also compares this portrait to the Copenhagen portrait of Vespasian.

[26] For example, a portrait found in Teate depicts a wreathed man with sunken cheeks, lined brow, and a protruding Adam's apple. At first identified as Nerva, the portrait is now dated to the 50s–40s B.C.E. (Museo Archeologico Nazionale, Chieti, inv. 8601; Di Mino and Nista 1993, cat no. 11, pp. 56–57 and Tav. XIII). See also a fragmentary, mid-first century B.C.E. portrait from Alba Fucens with a deeply furrowed brow and small, heavily lidded eyes (Museo Archeologico Nazionale, Chieti inv. 9679, Di Mino and Nista 1993, cat no. 10, pp. 54–55 and Tav. XII). Two full-length nude figures, also found in Foruli, share similar, if less intensely aged portrait features, including small, recessed eyes and lined foreheads, despite their disparate stylistic dates (60–50 B.C.E. for the older-looking figure; Julio-Claudian era for the younger-looking one). Museo Archeologico Nazionale, Chieti inv. 4428 and 4429, respectively; Di Mino and Nista 1993, cat. no. 1 and 2, pp. 36–39, Tav. I–IV, with previous bibliography. Torelli (2009) links these latter two figures with the Mucii Scaevolae.

[27] Museo Archeologico Nazionale, Chieti, inv. 8603. Limestone, 0.43 m. mid-first century B.C.E., from Teate; Di Mino and Nista 1993, cat. no. 12, pp. 58–59, Tav. XIV.

[28] See Dench (1995, 103–7) and Farney (2007, 206–10) on common mythical origins and later Roman conflation of Sabines and Samnites.

[29] Copenhagen, Ny Carlsberg Glyptothek, inv. 2116. Marble, 0.26 m. Poulsen (1962, cat. no. 27, pp. 58–59, pl. XXXIX) suggests that the portrait is "provincial" in style but that it could be an imperial-era copy of a Republican type. Johansen (1994, cat no. 28, pp. 80–81) identifies the date as "Original: Second half of the 1st cent. B.C." Cf. Ny Carlsberg Glyptothek, inv. 1666; Johansen 1994, cat. no. 108, pp. 240–41, a damaged travertine portrait of a man with similar small eyes, lined brow, and chin profile, supposedly found in the Sabine mountains and dated to the end of the first century B.C.E.

[30] According to the Johansen 1994, 80 catalogue: "Acquired in 1907, through the mediation of Helbig, from Anfidena in Samnium."

[31] Museo del Sannio, Benevento, inv. 634. Limestone, 1.07 x 0.87 x 0.24 m. Frenz 1985, cat no. 101, pp. 131, Taf. 42.1. Frenz dates the relief to the Claudian era.

[32] See Zanker 1979, 362–63 on imperial portraiture and Italian provincial styles and Croz 1996 on the possibility of a realistic "municipal elite" portrait style.

[33] This choice may be echoed in the selective "good" emperors—Augustus, Tiberius, and Claudius—listed in the *Lex de imperio Ves-*

pasiani (*CIL* 6 930 = *ILS* 244), as several scholars have suggested. See Brunt 1977 and Hurlet 1993 with further bibliography.

[34] On purposeful humility as an ideological stance, see Levick 2005, 65 and 76. On Vitellius's mythological descent from Faunus: Suet. *Vit.* 1. Vespasian's support for Galba may have also factored into the Flavians's early ideology, considering Galba's references to the Republican past in his lineage, numismatic portraits, and adoption of Piso; see Levick 2005, 72–73.

References

de Angelis, F., J.-A. Dickmann, F. Pirson, and R. von den Hoff, eds. 2012. *Kunst von unten?: Stil und Gesellschaft in der antiken Welt von der "arte plebea" bis heute*. Wiesbaden: Ludwig Reichert.

Beard, M. 2014. *Laughter in Ancient Rome. Sather Classical Lectures.* Vol. 71. Berkeley: University of California Press.

Bergmann, M., and P. Zanker. 1981. "'Damnatio Memoriae': Umgearbeitete Nero- und Domitansporträts: Zur Ikonographie der flavischen Kaiser und des Nerva." *JdI* 96:317–412.

Brunt, P.A. 1977. "Lex de Imperio Vespasiani." *JRS* 67:95–116.

Clarke, J.R. 2003. *Art in the Lives of Ordinary Romans: Visual Representation and Non-Elite Viewers in Italy, 100 B.C.–A.D. 315.* Berkeley: University of California Press.

Cox, S.E. 2014. "Innovative Antiquarianism: The Flavian Reshaping of the Past." *Attitudes towards the Past in Antiquity: Creating Identities.* edited by B. Alroth and C. Scheffer, 243–54. Stockholm Studies in Classical Archaeology 14. Stockholm: Stockholm University.

Croz, J-F. 1996. "Le visage des élites. Remarques sur les portraits de notables municipaux des Gracques à Néron. Quelques exemples des collections américaines et européennes." In *Les élites municipales de l'Italie péninsulaire des Gracques à Néron,* edited by M. Cébeillac-Gervasoni, 255–62. Naples: Centre Jean Bérard and Rome: Ecole française de Rome.

Daltrop, G., U. Hausmann, and M. Wegner. 1966. *Die Flavier: Vespasian, Titus, Domitian, Nerva, Julia Titi, Domitilla, Domitia.* Das römische Herrscherbild, 2.1. Berlin: Gebr. Mann.

Dench, E. 1995. *From Barbarians to New Men: Greek, Roman, and Modern Perceptions of Peoples of the Central Apennines.* Oxford: Oxford University Press.

———. 2005. *Romulus' Asylum: Roman Identities from the Age of Alexander to the Age of Hadrian.* Oxford: Oxford University Press.

Di Mino, M.R. and L. Nista, eds. 1993. *Gentes et Principes: Iconografia Romana in Abruzzo.* Chieti: Ministero per i Beni Culturali e Ambientali, Soprintendenza Archeologica dell'Abruzzo.

Farney, G.D. 2007. *Ethnic Identity and Aristocratic Competition in Republican Rome.* Cambridge: Cambridge University Press.

———. 2011. "Aspects of the Emergence of Italian Identity in the Early Roman Empire." *Communicating Identity in Italic Iron Age Communities*, edited by M. Gleba and H.W. Horsnæs, 223–32. Oxford: Oxbow Books.

Farney, G.D. and G. Masci. 2018. "The Sabines." In *The Peoples of Ancient Italy*, edited by G. Farney and G. Bradley, 543–57. Boston: Walter de Gruyter.

Farrell, J. 2014. "The Roman *Suburbium* and the Roman Past." In *Valuing the Past in the Greco-Roman World: Proceedings from the Penn-Leiden Colloquia on Ancient Values, VII*, edited by J. Ker and C. Pieper, 83–108. Leiden: E. J. Brill.

Frenz, H.G. 1985. *Römische Grabreliefs in Mittel- und Süditalien.* Rome: L'Erma di Bretschneider.

Gallia, A.B. 2012. *Remembering the Roman Republic: Culture, Politics, and History under the Principate.* Cambridge: Cambridge University Press.

Gruen, E.S. 1992. *Culture and National Identity in Republican Rome.* Ithaca, NY: Cornell University Press.

Hoff, R. von den. 2007. "Naturalism and Classicism: Style and Perception of Early Hellenistic Portraits." In *Early Hellenistic Portraiture: Image, Style, Context*, edited by R. von den Hoff and P. Schultz, 49–62. Cambridge: Cambridge University Press.

Hurlet, F. 1993. "La 'Lex de imperio Vespasiani' et la légitimité augustéenne." *Latomus* 52:261–80.

———. 2016. "Sources and Evidence." In *A Companion to the Flavian Age of Imperial Rome*, edited by A. Zissos, 17–39. Chichester: John Wiley & Sons.

Johansen, F. 1994. *Catalogue: Roman Portraits I.* Copenhagen: Ny Carlsberg Glyptotek.

———. 1995. *Catalogue: Roman Portraits II.* Copenhagen: Ny Carlsberg Glyptotek.

Kockel, V. 1993. *Porträtreliefs stadtrömischer Grabbauten: Ein Beitrag zur Geschichte und zum Verständnis des spätrepublikanisch-frühkaiserzeitlichen Privatporträts.* Mainz: Philipp von Zabern.

La Rocca, E. and C. Parisi Presicce, with A. Lo Monaco, eds. 2011. *Ritratti: Le Tante Facce del Potere.* Rome: MondoMostre.

Levick, B. 2005. *Vespasian.* London: Routledge.

Marlowe, E. 2013. *Shaky Ground: Context, Connoisseurship and the History of Roman Art.* London: Bloomsbury.

Panciera, S., and Zanker, P. 1988–1989. "Il ritratto e l'iscrizione di L. Licinius Nepos." *AttiPontAcc* 61:357–84.

Petersen, L.H. 2006. *The Freedman in Roman Art and Art History.* Cambridge: Cambridge University Press.

Pollini, J. 2007. "Ritualizing Death in Republican Rome: Memory, Religion, Class Struggle, and the Wax Ancestral Mask Tradition's Origin and Influence on Veristic Portraiture." In *Performing Death: Social Analyses of Funerary Traditions in the Ancient Near East and Mediterranean.*, edited by N. Laneri, 237–85. Oriental Institute Seminars 3. Chicago: The Oriental Institute of the University of Chicago.

Poulsen, V. 1962. *Les Portraits Romains.* Vol. 1, *République et dynastie Julienne.* Copenhagen: Ny Carlsberg Glyptotek.

Rolfe, J.C. 1998. *Suetonius. Lives of the Caesars.* Rev. ed. Cambridge, MA: Harvard University Press.

Rose, C.B. 2008. "Forging Identity in the Roman Republic: Trojan Ancestry and Veristic Portraiture." In *Role Models in the Roman World: Identity and Assimilation*, edited by S. Bell and I.L. Hansen, 97–131. Memoirs of the American Academy in Rome, Supplementary Volume 7. Ann Arbor: University of Michigan Press.

Rosso, E. 2009a. "Le thème de la *Res publica restituta* dans le monnayage de Vespasien: pérennité du 'modèle augustéen' entre citations, réinterprétations et dévoiements." In *Le principat d'Auguste. Réalités et représentations du pouvoir Autour de la Res publica restituta*, edited by F. Hurlet and B. Mineo, 209–42. Rennes: Presses universitaires de Rennes.

———. 2009b. "Cat. 1: Ritratto di Vespasiano." In *Divus Vespasianus: Il bimillenario dei Flavi*, edited by F. Coarelli, 402–3. Milano: Electa.

Torelli, M. 2009. "Il ciclo di ritratti dei Mucii Scaevolae da Foruli (Amiternum): un paradigma indiziario di prosopografia tra repubblica ed impero." *Maxima debetur magistro reverentia: Essays on Rome and the Roman Tradition in Honor of Russell T. Scott. Biblioteca di Athenaeum 54*, edited by P.B. Harvey, Jr. and C. Conybeare, 207–29. Como: New Press Edizioni.

Tuck, S.L. 2016. "Imperial Image-Making." In *A Companion to the Flavian Age of Imperial Rome.* edited by A. Zissos, 109–28. Chichester, UK: John Wiley & Sons.

Varner, E.R. 2004. *Mutilation and Transformation: Damnatio Memoriae and Roman Imperial Portraiture.* Leiden: E. J. Brill.

Wiseman, T.P. 1971. *New Men in the Roman Senate, 139 B.C.–A.D. 14.* Oxford: Oxford University Press.

Wood, S. 2016. "Public Images of the Flavian Dynasty: Sculpture and Coinage." In *A Companion to the Flavian Age of Imperial Rome.* edited by A. Zissos, 129–47. Chichester, UK: John Wiley & Sons.

Woodman, A.J., and R.H. Martin. 1996. *The Annals of Tacitus, Book 3.* Cambridge: Cambridge University Press.

Zanker, P. 1976. "Zur Rezeption des hellenistischen Individualporträts in Rom und in den italischen Städten." In *Hellenismus in Mittelitalien 1: Kolloquium in Göttingen vom 5. bis 9. Juni*

1974, edited by P. Zanker, 581–619. Göttingen: Vanden-
hoeck & Ruprecht.

———. 1979. "Prinzipat und Herrscherbild." *Gymnasium* 86: 353–
68.

New Observations on the Three Arches at Benevento

Gretel Rodríguez

Abstract

The Arch of Trajan at Benevento is well known to scholars of Roman art and architecture thanks to its excellent preservation and complex iconographic program. This paper explores the Arch of Trajan in its urban context, considering it as a group with two other arches that stood in the forum of Benevento. By revising the dates of construction for the three monuments and highlighting funerary elements in the iconography of the Arch of Trajan, I bring attention to a period of intense urbanization the city experienced at the turn of the second century C.E., and to the role of freestanding arches as shapers of the urban landscapes of ancient Roman cities.[1]

A FREESTANDING ARCH HONORING THE EMPEROR TRAJAN stands at the northeast access to the city of Benevento in Central Italy. Dedicated by the Senate and the People of Rome sometime around 114 C.E., the monument features a complex decorative program that highlights the figure of the emperor, who appears in a series of scenes depicting imperial functions and virtues. Since its restoration in the late nineteenth century, numerous studies have focused attention on the design and messages of the arch. The majority of those studies have considered the monument in isolation, usually disregarding its possible connections with the surrounding built environment. In this paper, I address the Arch of Trajan in combination with two other arches erected around the same time to explore their role as a group in shaping the urban image of ancient Benevento. I suggest that, rather than an isolated case of imperial commemoration, the Arch of Trajan was part of a larger program of construction that took place during the early second century C.E.

Architectural monuments were one of the ways ancient Romans employed to construct the public image of imperial authority, and freestanding arches were particularly efficient to accomplish that goal. Arches could be erected in a relatively short period of time and with minimal resources.[2] They could be sited at locations where the lack of space presented logistical problems.[3] With their relatively simple form, arches served as support for the placement of statues and reliefs, allowing patrons to transmit multiple messages simultaneously. This versatility constituted one of the strengths of freestanding arches as a type of honorific monument, a trait that ensured their proliferation throughout the empire for more than five centuries.[4] Besides the well-known Arch of Trajan at Benevento and the arch honoring the same emperor at the port of the city of Ancona, there is evidence for numerous additional arches associated with Trajan throughout Italy and the rest of the empire;[5] the two arches that stand in the forum of Benevento were possibly also part of this group.

An Urban Image of Benevento

The modern city of Benevento lies in an inner valley of the Campanian Apennines between the rivers Calore and Sabato, a strategic mountain pass that was as important for land communications in antiquity as it is today. Ancient Beneventum, which was home to the Hirpini, a branch of the Samnite tribe, became a Latin colony in 268 B.C.E. and a *municipium* in 90 B.C.E.[6] Despite its strategic location and importance in antiquity, not much is known of the later development of the city. The few Roman monuments that survive are in fragmentary state and poorly documented, with the exception of the single-bayed arch dedicated to Trajan, placed at the beginning of the Via Traiana (fig. 1). Excavations at Benevento have been intermittent, and the complex history of the town after the Roman period prevents a clear understanding of its urban topography.[7] A series of events in the post-Roman period complicate this scenario, including the devastating effects of several earthquakes, floods, and the sacking of the city by Goths in the fifth century and by Visigoths in the sixth.[8] The Lombards established the capital of their principate in Benevento between the sixth and the eleventh centuries, dramatically transforming the urban matrix and engaging in a systematic reuse of ancient architectural elements.[9] Despite the fragmentary nature of the investigations conducted at the site, some information can be gleaned by combining the archaeological record, the epigraphical and literary sources, and

Fig. 1. Benevento, Arch of Trajan (photo by the author).

what remains of the ancient topography in the modern city's layout.

As an important crossroads since pre-Roman times, Benevento was the natural confluence of several roads. The Via Appia, coming from Capua, entered the city through the west and possibly became one of the city's *decumani*.[10] The Via Latina also traversed the center of the city, as did roads that gave access to the upper Sannio and Avellino. Other critical roads that crossed the city were the Via Aemilia (second century B.C.E.), the Via Gellia (first century B.C.E.), the Via Aurelia Aeclanensis, and the Via Minucia.[11] Thanks to this network of roads, the city functioned as a key transitional point between northern and southern Italy, and, unlike other veteran settlements in central Italy, it continued to thrive after the civil war of the 80s B.C.E.[12] The three arches that survived in the city, as is commonly the case with this type of monument, were all connected with these roads in some way.

Archaeological remains at Benevento reveal an urban center that, although small, boasted a great number of large-scale buildings. The extension of the city in Roman times has been calculated to approximately one mile along the *decumanus maximus*.[13] The ancient forum—today the area between the Duomo and the Piazza Cardinale Pacca—was surrounded

Fig. 2. Benevento, city plan (Via Appia in red). (1) Arco del Sacramento; (2) "Arco"; (3) Forum; (4) Theater (modified after Google Maps, 2018).

by a series of large structures that archaeologists have identified as temples and civic buildings (fig. 2).[14] Among the remains are a temple possibly dedicated to Jupiter, a *macellum* (market), and two monumental arches.[15] Epigraphic evidence reveals the presence of temples elsewhere in the city dedicated to Vesta (first century B.C.E.), Hercules, and Mater Matuta.[16] The city's infrastructure included an unusually large number of baths, which suggests a substantial population living in rented *insulae*.[17] During the first decades of the second century, the city grew considerably with the addition of several ambitious projects. They included a theater with sufficient cavea capacity for more than seven thousand spectators and an amphitheater, now destroyed, located near the city walls.[18] In the western sector of the city, archaeologists have uncovered abundant ceramic evidence to suggest the presence of a manufacturing district, which went through a period of significant renovations in the early second century.[19] The erection of the two arches in the forum and the Arch of Trajan seems to coincide with this period of urban development.

The Arch of Trajan

The arch of Trajan was located just outside of the city walls of Benevento, at the outset of the Via Traiana. It was built with a core of local limestone lined with Parian marble, and its design echoes that of the Arch of Titus in Rome (fig. 3).[20]

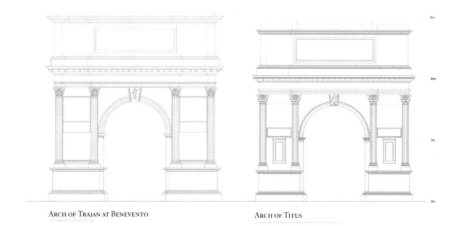

ARCH OF TRAJAN AT BENEVENTO   ARCH OF TITUS

The structure has most surfaces covered in reliefs. There are eight panels on the piers, divided by smaller friezes with allegorical motifs, two large panels on the inside of the bay, four panels on the attic, and a frieze that encircles the four sides. The spandrels and keystones feature allegorical figures. The lateral facades were plain, except for the frieze, the molded cornices, and two rectangles that likely contained painted inscriptions. The events depicted in the reliefs range from the prosaic to the allegorical. They include colonial foundations, the sealing of alliances, celebrations of commerce, sacrifices, and the traditional departures to and arrivals from wars.[21] In some of the scenes, the mortal emperor interacts with personifications and deities. He accepts the surrender of personified provinces and is crowned by Victory in the arch's vault. On the attic, facing the city, he stands across Jupiter, who extends his thunderbolt to Trajan, in what appears to be a symbolic transferring of power, a rather transgressive expression of imperial authority (fig. 4). The triumphal frieze likely represents Trajan's triumph over Dacia of 107 C.E.[22] The inscription on the attic suggests the year 114 for the dedication of the monument, when Trajan had been a Tribune for the eighteenth time and had received a seventh imperial salutation.[23] The arch was probably vowed after the Dacian triumph of 107 and completed during the following years.

Although multiple hypotheses have been advanced, the specific circumstances of the dedication of the Arch of Trajan at Benevento remain unclear. Neither the dedicatory inscription nor the ancient sources provide a definitive solution on the specific motivations for building the arch. Scholars have

Fig. 3. Comparative view of the arches of Titus in Rome and Trajan at Benevento (drawing by Bruno Rodríguez).

65

Fig. 4. Benevento, Arch of Trajan, detail of attic relief with Jupiter (city side) (photo by the author).

advanced various possibilities. Both Petersen (1892) and von Domaszewski (1899) suggested that the arch served as a celebration of Trajan's virtues as emperor. Paul Veyne emphasized the arch's funerary connotations proposing that the attic panels, different in style from those in the piers, commemorated the return of Trajan's ashes to Rome by his successor Hadrian.[24] Franz Hassel focused on the similarities between the Arch of Trajan and the Arch of Titus in Rome, and both he and Mario Rotili saw the arch as a commemoration of the inauguration of the Via Traiana.[25] For Mario Torelli, the sole purpose of the arch was the celebration of the *institutio alimentaria*, a cash distribution scheme dedicated to the welfare of children that Trajan implemented in Italy, which seems to have benefitted the inhabitants of Benevento.[26] De Maria considers the messages of the arch as purposely ambiguous, rejecting the need for a unilateral interpretation.[27] Several scholars have proposed a Hadrianic date for the monument, based on the differences in style between the reliefs of the piers and those on the attic, and the fact that Hadrian seems

Fig. 5. Benevento, Arco del Sacramento (photo by the author).

to appear next to Trajan in at least one of the reliefs.[28] Another hypothesis suggests that the arch—like the Forum of Trajan in Rome—was built as a symbolic gesture to muster support for Trajan's upcoming Parthian campaign.[29] Regardless of the specific circumstances that led to the construction of the Arch of Trajan, one aspect that these studies have omitted in their discussion is the place the monument occupies in the urban landscape of Benevento. As I explore below, there are possible associations between the Arch of Trajan and the two lesser-known arches that stood in the city.

Two Arches in the Forum of Benevento

Of these two arches, the one that is better preserved is known as the "Arco del Sacramento." It stands at the southwest end of the ancient forum, straddling the modern street, Via Carlo Torre (fig. 5). All that remains of the single-bayed structure is the brick-lined core, the travertine socle (now restored), and a few fragments of the original marble revetment.[30] Each pier has a niche set into each one of the long facades—likely to support statues—and a structural arch is still visible within the attic. The lack of surviving decoration or text makes the dating of the monument uncertain, but the construction technique suggests a date during the late Trajanic or early

Fig. 6. Benevento, forum arch ("arco") (photo by the author).

Hadrianic reigns.[31] The location of this structure, flanking the forum on its southeast side, suggests that the arch could have functioned as an access point to the piazza, although its orientation runs contrary to the Via Appia, which entered the city from the west.

A second arch stands west of the Arco del Sacramento and is aligned with the ancient Via Appia (fig. 6). The structure, which is sometimes called "Arco" and most times ignored in topographical and architectural surveys of Benevento, has suffered significant damage over the centuries. It was incorporated into the city walls during the Lombard period, bombarded during the second World War, and is now engulfed by modern construction.[32] It is also a single-bay arch built of brick-lined concrete, and like its neighbor, features a pair of niches, this time placed on the inner walls of the bay.[33] Clamp holes in the bricks suggest that the monument was lined with marble in antiquity. Like the Arco del Sacramento, the lack of surviving text or decoration prevents an accurate dating of the arch, which remains an enigmatic presence within the urban matrix of Benevento. Yet its location, aligned with the Via Appia and guarding one of the principal accesses to the forum, suggests it had greater importance in antiquity.

The dating of both the Arco del Sacramento and the unnamed arch rests upon the similarities that scholars have

noted between the *opus latericium* (brick-faced concrete) of the two arches and that of the Theater of Benevento, which has been dated to around 126 C.E. (fig. 7).[34] The date of the theater, however, relies on an inscription at the base of an honorific statue that once stood inside, but which was moved and reused during a later reconstruction.[35] The brickwork alone would suggest a broader range, to include between the late first and the early second centuries C.E., corresponding to the Trajanic and early Hadrianic reigns.[36] Expanding the date range for the two arches in the forum allows us to view them as part of the same process of intense urbanization that the city of Benevento experienced at the turn of the second century. In combination with the Arch of Trajan, these monuments also exemplify how freestanding arches were used to shape spaces and control circulation in ancient Benevento.

Fig. 7 . Benevento, Theater (photo by the author).

As studies of Roman and provincial arches demonstrate, these monuments were key in the construction of urban narratives, to articulate spatial meanings and to express individual agendas. In cities like Pompeii, for instance, arches regulated access to public spaces such as the forum.[37] The same happened in Rome, where, over centuries, arches gradually shaped the image and circulation behaviors in the Roman Forum and its surroundings.[38] Also in the capital, arches were used to define and map the triumphal route.[39] At Benevento, the two forum arches had a similar function. They were closely connected with the piazza and the buildings around it, framing the roads that entered the city. The unnamed arch coincides with the east–west orientation of the earliest tracing of the Via Appia, modern Via San Filippo, which suggests that it could have been built at an earlier date to conform to the road. If so, the arch functioned as a monumental access to Benevento for visitors coming from Rome. In contrast, the Arco del Sacramento, facing northeast and oriented almost at a 90-degree angle with respect to the previous arch, saddles the current Via Carlo Torre, which in antiquity flanked the forum area on the east; in this position it allows communication between the forum proper and the theater district to the south. Together, the two arches possibly created a seamless flow within the forum space. The Arch of Trajan, by contrast, stood at a distance from the city center, right outside the ancient *pomerium*. It was then similar to other provincial arches, which served as real or symbolic gateways and possibly possessed apotropaic connotations.[40] The Arch of Trajan was also a memorial for the emperor. All visitors, both arriving from the east or departing from town, had to pass under or around the structure, engaging with its persuasive imagery. Erected in an area of the city that was mostly unbuilt,[41] the arch stood in relative isolation, but its connection with the Via Traiana turned it into a billboard that proclaimed Benevento's role as an essential junction between northern and southern Italy, and between the peninsula and Greece.

Funerary Allusions of the Arch of Trajan

The extra-urban location of the Arch of Trajan seems to betray other motivations. One hypothesis that attempts to explain the reasons for dedication of the arch is Paul Veyne's proposition that the monument, although possibly planned by Trajan, was completed by Hadrian as a posthumous honor to his adoptive father.[42] Although this interpretation has not been universally accepted, additional elements in the siting and design of the arch suppoert a funerary connotation. A first indication is its location outside the *pomerium*, the town's sacred boundary. In the Roman world, tombs were, by law, built outside city boundaries, often in association with access roads.[43] Provincial arches often stood on the periphery of cities, announcing as massive billboards their identity to visitors. If the primary function of the Arch of Trajan was

to commemorate Trajan's role in the *alimenta,* or if it constituted a general celebration of his emperorship, a location near
the forum would seem more appropriate, especially given the
construction boom the city center experienced around the
time of the arch's dedication. An extra-urban location for a
monument of such ambition—a dedication to the emperor
by senatorial decree—makes sense if the goal of the arch was
to monumentalize the new road. But the themes of the reliefs suggest also the possibility that the arch functioned as a
commemorative monument.[44] Other elements in the iconographic program—the attic scene where Jupiter offers his
thunderbolt to Trajan and the references to funerary rituals
in the smaller relief panels— also reinforce a funerary connotation.[45] Considering the arch as a funerary monument helps
explain the stylistic differences scholars have noticed between
the reliefs on the piers and those on the attic, which seem
to be later.[46] Perhaps more significantly, if we accept Veyne's
arguments, the Arch of Trajan becomes part of a larger urban narrative. During the early reign of Hadrian, Benevento
saw a period of intense monumentalization and regulariza-
tion of its urban spaces with the construction of buildings
like the theater, the amphitheater, and the two arches in the
forum.[47] The completion of the Arch of Trajan seems to have
been part of this process, which helped define the boundaries
of the city and monumentalized one of its principal points
of access. The monument was possibly vowed after the victory over Dacia in 107 and completed after Trajan's death in
117, during the early years of Hadrian's reign, while the two
arches in the forum were also being erected. In its elevated
position, at the pinnacle of ascent coming from the east along
the Via Traiana, the Arch of Trajan functioned as a monumental billboard that announced to visitors this new period
of urbanization.

* * *

The ancient city of Benevento was a small town with an
ambitious urban layout that played a significant role in communications within the Italian peninsula, and between Italy
and the eastern provinces. The emergence in the early second century of impressive public monuments, suggests that
the city was booming with development and maintained a
large urban population. The dedication of three arches, two
in the forum and one in the outskirts of the town, coincides
with this process, and speaks about the role of freestanding

arches in articulating urban spaces. The city's development seems to have responded to a concerted effort on the part of local magistrates, private citizens, and the Roman state, to boost the city's visibility as an urban center, capitalizing on its advantageous geographic position and the confluence of important communication routes. We can no longer tell what messages—if any—were transmitted by the visual program on the two arches in the forum. Viewing them as group with the Arch of Trajan, and judging by the exuberant imagery of the latter, they must have been an equally impressive sight in the urban matrix of ancient Benevento.

Notes

[1] This article grew from my doctoral dissertation, "The Dynamics of Roman Honorific Arches: Space, Design, and Reception" (University of Texas at Austin, 2018). I would like to express my deepest gratitude to my dissertation supervisors, John R. Clarke and Penelope J.E. Davies, for years of generous mentorship. I thank the editor of this volume, Francesco de Angelis, and the anonymous reviewers who helped improve the work with their insightful comments. I benefited from the feedback of those who read earlier drafts, including Nayla Muntasser, Nassos Papalexandrou, Andrew Riggsby, Meghan Rubenstein, Danilo Udovicki, and Robyn Walsh. My research in Benevento was funded in part by the Oplontis Project and the Center for the Study of Ancient Italy of the University of Texas at Austin.

[2] See Favro 2011, 357–58 for an estimate considering the Arch of Septimius Severus in the Roman Forum as a case study.

[3] See, for instance, the location of the Parthian Arch of Augustus, or the Arch of Septimius Severus in the Roman Forum.

[4] General studies on honorific and triumphal arches include Kähler 1939; Mansuelli 1954, 1979; Kleiner 1985, 1989; De Maria 1988; Gros 1996; Cassibry 2009, 2018.

[5] For a summary of arches built in honor of Trajan in Italy, see De Maria 1988, 340–43.

[6] Livy 9.27.14; *Per.* 15; Vell. Pat. 1.14.7; Torelli 2002.

[7] For excavations see De Franciscis 1948, 1951; Giampaola 1988, 1990; Marcello Rotili 1986, 2006.

[8] De Caro and Pontrandolfo 1981, 164; Marcello Rotili 2006, 18.

[9] Marcello Rotili 1986, 63 and passim; Giampaola 1990; Torelli 2002, 288 and passim.

[10] Marcello Rotili 1986, 27–28; Giampaola 1990, 285.

[11] Strabo 5.4.11; 6.3.7; Hor. *Ep.* 1.18.20; Torelli 2002, 106, 167.

[12] Torelli 2002, 164.

[13] Marcello Rotili 1986, 35. The *cardo maximus* seems to have coincided with the modern Via Traiano.

[14] De Franciscis 1948, 1951; Giampaola 1988, 1990; Marcello Rotili 1986.

[15] Suet. *Gramm.* 9, reports the presence of an statue of the grammarian Orbilius located in the city's Capitolium. Marcello Rotili 1986, 43–49; Torelli 2002, 110.

[16] Marcello Rotili 1986, 49 (Vesta), 50 (Mater Matuta), 37, 50 (Hercules).

[17] Marcello Rotili 1986, 35. Epigraphical evidence also attests to a *curator operis thermarum* active by the early second century C.E., Marcello Rotili 1986, 61.

[18] Lugli 1957, 515, pl. II; Giampaola 1990, 287; Sear 1993, 689–90.

[19] Marcello Rotili 2006, 22 and passim.

[20] The literature on the Arch of Trajan at Benevento is extensive. See primarily Meomartini 1889–1895; Petersen 1892; von Domaszewski 1899; Veyne 1960; Hassel 1966; Fittschen 1972; Gauer 1974; Mario Rotili 1972; Simon and Gawlikowski 1981; De Maria 1988, 232–35; Currie 1996; Torelli 1997.

[21] For analyses of the iconography, see Snijder 1926; Hamberg 1945; Pietrangeli 1947; Veyne 1960; Hassel 1966; Fittschen 1972; Mario Rotili 1972; Gauer 1974; Tomei 1976; Simon and Gawlikowski 1981; Currie 1996; Torelli 1997.

[22] According to Pliny the Younger, there were two triumphs after the Dacian campaigns, Plin. *Ep.* 8.4.2; With an indirect reference, see also Cass. Dio 68.15.

[23] *CIL* 9 1558. IMP CAESARI DIVI NERVAE FILIO // NERVAE TRAIANO OPTIMO AVG // GERMANICO DACICO PONTIF MAX TRIB // POTEST XVIII IMP VII COS VI P P // FORTISSIMO PRINCIPI SENATVS P Q R. Trajan received the title *Optimus* between August and December 114, De Maria 1988, 234.

[24] Veyne 1960.

[25] Hassel 1966, 8, 22, and passim; Mario Rotili 1972, esp. 55.

[26] Torelli 1997. On the *alimenta*, see Aur. Vict. *Caes.* 12.4; Duncan-Jones 1964; Woolf 1990; Rawson 2001, 24–25; Torelli 2002, 202–13.

[27] De Maria 1988, 129–30.

[28] Those who have identified a figure standing next to Trajan in the *profectio* scene of the city side attic with Hadrian are: Snijder 1926, 94–128; Hamberg 1945, 66; Pietrangeli 1947; Veyne 1960. Contra: Fittschen 1972, 777; Simon and Gawlikowski 1981, 10; Torelli 1997, esp. 170, n. 70.

[29] Hamberg 1945, 68–71; Lepper 1979; De Maria 1988, 128.

[30] Measurements: 11.20 long by 4.50 deep and 12 meters high. The central *fornix* measures 7.90 meters high by 5 meters long; De Maria 1988, 235.

[31] Hassel 1968; Marcello Rotili 1986, 41; De Maria 1988, 235.

[32] The structure is today abandoned. Among the few sources that

address this monument, see Marcello Rotili 1986, 41–42. De Maria does not include it in his catalogue of Roman arches in Italy.

[33] The structure rests upon a rectangular base measuring 10.50 by 6.30 meters.

[34] Lugli 1957, 597; De Caro and Pontrandolfo 1981, 188.

[35] Cavuoto 1969; Marcello Rotili 1986, 51.

[36] Blake 1973, 262–63; Giampaola (1990, n. 74) disputes the use of the bases for dating the monument. See also Sear 1993, 690 and n. 16.

[37] De Maria 1988, 58–60, 79–82.

[38] Favro 1996; Thomas 2001; Gorski and Packer 2015; Rodríguez 2018, 70–80.

[39] Östenberg 2009, 2010; Popkin 2016.

[40] The construction of arches was often associated with the foundation of cities and with the ritual definition of urban perimeters, Frothingham 1905, 1915; Scagliarini Corlàita 1979; De Maria 1988; Stevens 2017. These apotropaic functions at times merged with funerary connotations, see Mansuelli 1954, esp. 100–102; Richardson 1992, 22 and passim. Placed at liminal locations, arches offered protection for those passing under their structures, usually with the aid of representations of deities and other apotropaic devices; De Maria 1973, 36.

[41] Giampaola 1988, 830.

[42] Veyne 1960.

[43] Cic. Leg. 2.58.

[44] As defined by Frischer, for whom "the purpose of this kind of monument is to celebrate and commemorate a life devoted to civic virtue" (1982–1983, 84). He views them as distinct from tombs and cenotaphs, which marked the place of death or burial; but see Davies (2000, 179), who suggests the distinction is far from clear.

[45] See, for instance, the motif of Victories slaying bulls and the figures holding candelabra, which are associated with funerary culture in various contexts. For the *Victoria tauroctona* motif, see Mario Rotili 1972, 754; Jameson 2014. For candelabra, see Rushforth 1915.

[46] For stylistic analyses, see primarily Hamberg 1945, 63–75; Mario Rotili 1972.

[47] Giampaola 1990, 284–87; Torelli 2002, 213 and passim.

References

Blake, M.E. 1973. *Roman Construction in Italy from Nerva Through the Antonines*. Philadelphia: American Philosophical Society.

Cassibry, K.B. 2009. "The Allure of Monuments in the Roman Empire: Provincial Perspectives on the Triumphal Arch." Ph.D. diss., University of California, Berkeley.

———. 2018. "Reception of the Roman Arch Monument." *AJA* 122:245–75.

Cavuoto, P. 1969. "Le epigrafi del teatro romano di Benevento." *Rendiconti dell'Accademia Nazionale dei Lincei, Classe di scienze morali, storiche e filologiche* 24:87–99.

Currie, A. 1996. "The Empire of Adults: the Representation of Children on Trajan's Arch at Beneventum." In *Art and Text in Roman Culture*, edited by Jas Elsner, 153–81. Cambridge: Cambridge University Press.

Davies, P.J.E. 2000. *Death and the Emperor: Roman Imperial Funerary Monuments from Augustus to Marcus Aurelius*. Cambridge: Cambridge University Press.

De Caro, S., and A. Pontrandolfo. 1981. *Campania: guida archeologica*. Rome: Laterza.

De Franciscis, A. 1948. "Scoperte e saggi di scavo nell'area della citta (1947)." *Fasti Archeologici* 2:295.

———. 1951. "Beneventum, Benevento. Scavi." *Fasti Archeologici* 6:346–47.

De Maria, S. 1973. "Metodologia per una rilettura dei fornici di Roma antica." *Parametro* 20:36–41.

———. 1988. *Gli archi onorari di Roma e dell'Italia romana*. Rome: L'Erma di Bretschneider.

von Domaszewski, A. 1899. "Die politische Bedeutung des Traiansbogens in Benevent." *Jahreshefte des Österreichischen Archäologischen Institutes in Wien* 2:181–92.

Duncan-Jones, R. 1964. "The Purpose and Organization of the Alimenta." *PBSR* 32:123–46.

Favro, D. 1996. *The Urban Image of Augustan Rome*. Cambridge: Cambridge University Press.

———. 2011. "Construction Traffic in Imperial Rome: Building the Arch of Septimius Severus." In *Rome, Ostia, Pompeii: Movement and Space*, edited by R. Laurence and D.J. Newsome, 332–60. Oxford: Oxford University Press.

Fittschen, K. 1972. "Das Bildprogramm des Trajansbogens zu Benevent." *AA* 87:742–88.

Frischer, B. 1982–1983. "*Monumenta et Arae Honoris Virtutisque Causa*: Evidence of Memorials for Roman Civic Heroes." *Bullettino della Commissione Archeologica Comunale di Roma* 88:51–86.

Frothingham, A.L. Jr. 1905. "De la véritable signification des monuments romains qu'on appelle 'arcs de triomphe.'" *Revue Archéologique* 6:216–30.

———. 1915. "The Roman Territorial Arch." *AJA* 19:155–74.

Gauer, W. 1974. "Zum Bildprogramm des Trajansbogens von Benevent." *JDAI* 89:308–35.

Giampaola, D. 1988. "Il restauro dell'arco di Traiano e il resoconto dell'attività di scavo a Benevento." In *Poseidonia–Paestum: atti del ventisettesimo convegno di studi sulla Magna Grecia: Taranto-Paestum, 9–15 ottobre 1987*, 827–32. Taranto: Istituto per la storia e l'archeologia della Magna Grecia.

———. 1990. "Benevento: Il processo di aggregazione di un territorio." In *Basilicata: l'espansionismo romano nel sud-est d'Italia, il quadro archeologico. Atti del convegno, Venosa, 23–25 aprile 1987*, edited by M. Salvatore, 281–301. Venosa: Osanna Venosa.

Gorski, G., and J. E. Packer. 2015. *The Roman Forum: A Reconstruction and Architectural Guide*. Cambridge: Cambridge University Press.

Gros, P. 1996. *L'architecture romaine: du début du Iiieme Siècle Av. J.C. à la fin du haut-empire*. Paris: Picard.

Hamberg, P.G. 1945. *Studies in Roman Imperial Art*. Copenhagen: Munksgaard.

Hassel, F. J. 1966. *Der Trajansbogen in Benevent: Ein Bauwerk des römischen Senates*. Mainz: Philipp von Zabern.

———. 1968. "Zum Arco del Sacramento in Benevent." *Jahrbuch des Römisch-Germanischen Zentralmuseum Mainz* 15:95–98.

Jameson, M.H. 2014. *Cults and Rites in Ancient Greece: Essays on Religion and Society*. Cambridge: Cambridge University Press.

Kähler, H. 1939. "Triumphbogen (Ehrenbogen)." *Realencyclopadie der classischen Altertumswissenschaft* VII.A. 1:373–493.

Kleiner, F. S. 1985. *The Arch of Nero in Rome: A Study of the Roman Honorary Arch before and under Nero*. Rome: L'Erma di Bretschneider.

———. 1989. "The Study of Roman Triumphal and Honorary Arches 50 Years after Kähler." *JRA* 2:195–206.

Lepper, F.A. 1979. *Trajan's Parthian War*. Westport, CT: Greenwood Press.

Lugli, G. 1957. *La tecnica edilizia romana con particolare riguardo a Roma e Lazio: 1*. Rome: Giovanni Bardi.

Mansuelli, G.A., ed. 1954. "El arco honorífico en el desarrollo de la arquitectura romana." *Archivo Español de Arqueología* 27.89/90:93–178.

———. 1979. *Studi sull'arco onorario romano*. Rome: L'Erma di Bretschneider.

Meomartini, A. 1889–1895. *I monumenti e le opere d'arte della città di Benevento: lavoro storico, artistico, critico*. Benevento: Tipografia di L. de Martini e figlio.

Östenberg, I. 2009. *Staging the World: Spoils, Captives, and Representations in the Roman Triumphal Procession*. Oxford: Oxford University Press.

———. 2010. "*Circum metas fertur*: An Alternative Reading of the Triumphal Route." *Hist.* 59:303–20.

Petersen, E. 1892. "L'arco di Traiano a Benevento." *RM* 7:240–64.

Pietrangeli, C. 1947. *L'arco di Traiano a Benevento*. Novara: De Agostini.

Popkin, M.L. 2016. *The Architecture of the Roman Triumph: Monuments, Memory, and Identity*. Cambridge: Cambridge University Press.

Rawson, B. 2001. "Children as Cultural Symbols: Imperial Ideology in the Second Century." In *Childhood, Class and Kin in the Roman World*, edited by S. Dixon, 21–42. London: Routledge.

Richardson, L. Jr. 1992. *A New Topographical Dictionary of Ancient Rome*. Baltimore: Johns Hopkins University Press.

Rodríguez, G. 2018. "The Dynamics of Roman Honorific Arches: Space, Design, and Reception." Ph.D. diss., The University of Texas at Austin.

Rotili, Marcello. 1986. *Benevento romana e longobarda: l'immagine urbana*. Benevento: Banca sannitica.

———. 2006. *Benevento nella tarda antichità: dalla diagnostica archeologica in Contrada e Cellarulo alla ricostruzione dell'assetto urbano*. Naples: Arte Tipografica Editrice, 2006.

Rotili, Mario. 1972. *L'arco di Traiano a Benevento*. Rome: Instituto Poligrafico dello Stato, Libreria.

Rushforth, McN. 1915. "Funeral Lights in Roman Sepulchral Monuments." *JRS* 5:149–64.

Scagliarini Corlàita, D. 1979. "La situazione urbanistica degli archi onorari nella prima eta' imperiale." In *Studi sull'arco onorario romano*, edited by G. Mansuelli, 29–72. Rome: L'Erma di Bretschneider.

Sear, F.B. 1993. "The Scaenae Frons of the Theater of Pompey." *JRA* 97:687–701.

Simon, E., and M. Gawlikowski. 1981. *Die Götter am Trajansbogen zu Benevent*. Mainz: Philipp von Zabern.

Snijder, G. 1926. "Der Trajansbogen in Benevent: Bemerkungen zur Trajanischen und Hadrianischen Skulptur." *JdI* 41:94–128.

Stevens, S. 2017. *City Boundaries and Urban Development in Roman Italy*. Interdisciplinary Studies in Ancient Culture and Religion 16. Leuven: Peeters.

Thomas, M.L. 2001. "Constructing Dynastic Legitimacy: Imperial Building Programs in the Forum Romanum from Augustus to Diocletian." Ph.D. diss., University of Texas at Austin.

Tomei, M.A. 1976. "Osservazioni su alcune personificazioni femminili dell'arco di Traiano a Benevento." *Studi Miscellanei* 22:205–12.

Torelli, Marina R. 2002. *Benevento romana*. Rome: "L'Erma" di Bretschneider.

Torelli, Mario. 1997. "'Ex His Castra, Ex His Tribus Replebuntur': The Marble Panegyric on the Arch of Trajan at Beneventum." In *The Interpretation of Architectural Sculpture in Greece and Rome*, edited by D.B. Oliver, 144–71. Washington DC: National Gallery of Art.

Veyne, P. 1960. "Une hypothèse sur l'arc de Bénévent." *Mélanges d'Archéologie et d'Histoire* 72:191–219.

Woolf, G. 1990. "Food, Poverty, and Patronage: The Significance of the Epigraphy of the Roman Alimentary Schemes in Early

Imperial Italy." *Papers of the British School at Rome* 58:197–228.

In the Footsteps of Augustus: Hadrian and the Imperial Cult

Lillian Joyce

Abstract

Hadrian sought to honor, emulate and even surpass Augustus in a variety of his actions as Princeps. Associations with imperial cult were part of Hadrian's consolidation and unification of empire. Hadrian erected, revived, or enhanced at least twelve temples and shrines connected to imperial cult. I suggest adding the Temple of Venus and Roma to this list. Its Greek-style plan and choice of goddesses connected it to the legacy of Augustus. The goddesses Venus and Roma functioned effectively as surrogates for imperial cult with Venus as Augustus's divine ancestress and Roma as the cult consort of Augustus. In its use of Augustan models with associations to imperial cult and the power of the living emperor, the temple revealed Hadrian's sophisticated plan to showcase his power through a connection to the Augustan legacy and concepts of eternal empire.

HADRIAN'S GENERAL ADMIRATION FOR AUGUSTUS IS WELL known. This paper looks more closely at how Hadrian used emperor worship and in particular ties to the worship of Augustus to legitimize his succession, project power, unify peoples, and portend his senatorial designation as *divus*. The sites of Lugdunum and Tarraco in the west and Pergamon and Athens in the east are examined to assess how Hadrian's restorations and additions to Augustan worship sites played a key role in elevating Hadrian's status and securing the loyalty of disparate peoples. In addition to the restoration and construction of temples, the multiplication of altars and statues served as physical reminders of Hadrian's authority and sway. In Rome, where the Senate did not condone worship of a living emperor, Hadrian's innovative temple of Venus and Roma served as an ideal surrogate. Built in a commanding location in a decidedly "Greek" style, it evoked provincial temples of emperor worship. The choice of goddesses, reinforced by their colossal scale, also bolstered those associations, as Roma was the cult partner of Augustus and Venus the divine ancestress of Augustus' *gens*.

Since antiquity, sources have noted Hadrian's admiration for Augustus. Hadrian had a bust of Augustus among the Lares in his bedroom and a portrait of Augustus on his signet ring.[1] Beyond keeping these images of Augustus close to his person, Hadrian sought to honor, emulate, and even surpass the first emperor in a variety of actions. In 121, Hadrian proclaimed a new Golden Age, celebrating it with coins, games, and festivals.[2] Around 123, he shortened his title to *Hadrianus Augustus*.[3] He restored Augustan monuments within and outside of Rome, and began new projects, including the temple to Venus and Roma, which evoked Augustan symbols and were often tied to imperial cult. With these projects, Hadrian used the memory of Augustus as an innovative way to legitimize and promote himself.[4]

During the reign of Augustus, the endorsement of emperor worship and other honors was a complex affair. Augustus negotiated assertions of his power while also trying to appear decorous. He famously turned down some honors, while accepting others, such as command of the legions and the title of Pontifex Maximus, assuring his control of military and religious life. Suetonius maintained that Augustus sanctioned his own worship as long as it was in conjunction with Roma, the personification of the city and state of Rome.[5]

Subsequently, the Senate and various municipalities instituted imperial worship, providing local populations an opportunity to compete for imperial favor. Municipalities and individuals had considerable freedom in the way they honored the Emperor.[6] Nicolaus of Damascus observed, "Because men addressed him as Augustus in view of his claim to honour they revere him with temples and sacrifices over all the islands and continents, in cities and tribes requiting him for the magnitude of his virtue and his benefactions towards them."[7] The cult served to unify cultural, religious, and political practice.[8] But Augustus forbade state rites in Rome.[9] Nonetheless, he set the precedent for emperor worship throughout the land. More sanctuaries were devoted to Augustus than to any of his successors.[10] Hadrian in turn surpassed Augustus in the number of altars dedicated to him.[11] Athens set up over 100 altars to Hadrian.[12] Associations with Augustus and emperor worship were part of Hadrian's consolidation and unification of empire and he used symbolism and ritual to establish imperial identity, his legitimacy, and ultimately his legacy.

While imperial cult had persisted from the time of Augustus, subsequent emperors pursued it with less fervor and fewer sites of devotion. Hadrian embraced the practice by erecting, reviving, and enhancing multiple temples and shrines with connections to emperor worship.[13] In 121, after proclaiming the Golden Age and transforming the Parilia, the birthday celebrations of Rome, to the Rhomaia festival for the goddess Roma, Hadrian set out to tour the provinces.[14] During his travels, Hadrian's acts of munificence, remarkable in number and generosity, further established a link to Augustus.[15] In following his journeys we can establish the connection to Hadrian's particular use of imperial cult as well its ties to Augustus, and in particular to Augustus's worship while living. As a sample of these practices, I will briefly examine two sites in the east and two in the west that have significance as Augustan-period foundations subsequently enhanced and amplified by Hadrian's interventions. Lugdunum, the first altar of emperor worship in the west, later underwent a Hadrianic restoration with the establishment of a temple. Tarraco had an altar and then the first western temple of imperial cult that Tacitus (*Ann.* 1.78) framed as "precedent setting." Pergamon, where Augustus wintered in 29 B.C.E., was among the initial sites of emperor worship in the east, again establishing a standard, later augmented by Hadrian. In Athens, Hadrian's worship connected to and surpassed that of Augustus. Finally, I will explore Hadrianic allusions to emperor worship in Rome.

In the Hellenistic era in the east, few temples to rulers were built. Only two or three of the dozen shrines had temples.[16] Still, the Greek world had a tradition of honoring living rulers and conquerors. Starting in the early second century B.C.E., the Greeks erected shrines for the deity Roma, beginning in Smyrna.[17] In the west, no precedent existed for emperor worship or state-associated deities such as Roma. Augustus introduced the practice. Drusus established the earliest western altar to Roma and Augustus in 12 B.C.E. at Lugdunum. The altar had an enormous 50 m base and its appearance survives in numerous coin images (fig. 1).[18] Hadrian restored the Victoria columns with Egyptian syenite.[19] Interestingly, after he sponsored a new temple near the altar, inscriptional references to the altar temporarily stopped. The Hadrianic temple for

Roma and the Augusti (the current emperor and the deified dead) became the center of cult activity.[20] In this way, Hadrian introduced the first major change to imperial cult practice at Lugdunum since the time of Augustus.[21] In 121 Hadrian likely wanted to establish and affirm his legitimacy. Imperial cult and a symbolic link to Augustus suited his agenda well.[22]

When Hadrian wintered in Tarraco in 122–123, he restored the Temple of Augustus with his own funds.[23] Augustus had recuperated here in 26–25 B.C.E. and used it as a de facto capital.[24] Imperial worship began with a municipal altar of Augustus.[25] The locals may have learned from the example of Mytilene when the latter sent an embassy to Tarraco seeking approval to build a temple to Augustus and Roma.[26] Early in the reign of Tiberius, Tacitus recorded that Tarraco dedicated a temple.[27] Tacitus also noted that this temple was intended as an example for all provinces to follow.[28] Coins after 22 C.E. display two temple types, one Italic and one Greek.[29] Reverses with the Italic temple vary in details whereas the three-step, Greek-style temple is constant in appearance.[30] The Greek-style temple aligned with the appearance of such temples in the East and is possibly the style Tarraco chose.[31] In the west, it is possible that the peripteral temple was not merely a reference to "Greekness," but a type associated with imperial cult. Tarraco envisioned Augustus as Jupiter enthroned—bare-chested with globus, Victoria, and spear— also an eastern model.[32]

The first item in the *Historia Augusta* regarding Tarraco is that Hadrian used his own funds to rebuild the temple of Augustus.[33] Hadrian also called for a gathering of the Council of the Province, which administered the imperial cult. The likely meeting spot was close to the site of the temple. Thus, the ceremonial backdrop for meeting these representatives was the site of the imperial cult celebrating Augustus. Locals soon

began to add images of Hadrian to the sanctuary and a high priest received a mandate from the Council to gild Hadrian's statues. Locals carried these images during festivals and then kept them in the porch of the temple.[34]

While Hadrian's exact route through the Iberian Peninsula is not known, Birley maintained it is probable that he followed the route of Augustus.[35] The *Historia Augusta* is selective in its remarks on Hadrian's travels. Tarraco merited mention. Hadrian was able to use the potency of this site to align himself with the Augustan legacy.[36] It was also the 150th anniversary of Octavian taking the title Augustus and the time when Hadrian's coinage shortened his title to "Hadrianus Augustus."[37]

In 123 Hadrian journeyed east,[38] where a more developed tradition of emperor worship was in place. Cities competed to have a provincial temple to the emperor.[39] Pergamon was the first city to earn *neokoros* standing twice.[40] Its earlier temple was to Augustus and Roma. Founded in 29 B.C.E., Dio Cassius recorded that it was the first provincial temple for use by "Hellenes" rather than Romans.[41] Asia had backed Antony; thus, securing the provincial temple to Augustus and Roma helped affirm their support of the new leader.[42] Additionally, Augustus granted Pergamon sacred games, an honor seemingly omitted for the other provincial temple in Nikomedia.[43] The second Pergamene temple was to Trajan and Zeus Philios, with the epithet signaling the bond of alliance and, as Burrell argued, "presaging the identification of Hadrian with Zeus *Olympios* and *Eleutherios* throughout the

Fig. 2. Obverse: Trajan and Zeus Philios. Reverse: Augustus and Roma. Pergamon, 113/4 C.E.; BMC 263–265, Medals and Antiquities B 453 (Bibliothèque nationale de France).

Greek world."[44] Correspondence regarding the temple dates from 114 to 116, near the end of Trajan's life.[45] Inscriptions concerning the festivals follow the same formula as those of Roma and Augustus.[46] A bronze series celebrating the second neokorate depicts this new temple on its obverse with the Augustan temple on its reverse (fig. 2).[47] A seated Zeus receives the standing Trajan; while on the reverse, the now regularly employed Roma crowning Augustus in a cuirass appears. Remains of three colossal acrolithic sculptures were found in the vaults below the cella. A fragmentary inscription recorded that Hadrian had turned down a Pergamene request for a temple and instead proclaimed that his *eikon* be placed in the temple with his father (fig. 3). The inscription does not use the term *agalma*, which would have been more appropriate for a cult image, but the images of the two emperors were virtually identical.[48] While the interactions of Hadrian in Pergamon acknowledged his immediate predecessor, Trajan, the references also stressed connections to Augustus and Roma through architecture, statuary, ritual, and coinage.

Fig. 4. Temple of Venus and Roma, Rome (Carole Raddato).

In Athens, the Augustus-Hadrian link also was strong. The Athenians dedicated a temple to Augustus and Roma on the Acropolis.[49] This round structure was directly in front of the eastern entrance to the Parthenon.[50] However, in scale it did not visually dominate the Parthenon or the Acropolis landscape. This connection had been in place for well over 100 years when Hadrian arrived.[51] Like Augustus, Hadrian was initiated into the Eleusinian Mysteries.[52] We know of multiple benefactions throughout the city much like those of Augustus.[53] One was finishing the Olympieion. Suetonius recorded Augustus's unrealized plans to complete it and dedicate it to his Genius.[54] When accomplished by Hadrian in 131, it was the largest temple in Greece and housed a colossal, chryselephantine image of Zeus.[55] Inside the precinct, the Athenians dedicated a colossal statue of Hadrian and bases for at least 29 other statues of Hadrian are still extant.[56] This temple had strong associations with Hadrian and imperial cult even though his image did not share the cella with Zeus.[57] Pausanias (1.24.7) also saw a statue of Hadrian in the Parthenon. Additionally, Hadrian received honors as "Panhellenios," creating an institution, cult center, and games celebrating Greekness and loyalty to Rome centered in Athens.[58]

In 125 Hadrian was in Rome again. It is likely that the rebuilding of the Pantheon would have been complete.

Fig. 5. Obverse: Aureus of Hadrian. Reverse: ROMA AETERNA with victory. Rome mint, 134–138, RIC 2 263A (© Trustees of the British Museum).

Although seemingly begun during the latter part of Trajan's reign, Hadrian was its end user and ultimate determiner of functions.[59] If we look at the Pantheon's origins, Dio Cassius noted that Agrippa originally wanted the structure to be an Augusteum, but that Augustus rejected this designation.[60] Dio Cassius also recorded that the niches in the porch contained images of Augustus and Agrippa and that an image of Julius Caesar was inside with Venus and Mars. As La Rocca has recently suggested, "the potential for divinization was implicit in placing the statues of Agrippa and Augustus in the porch."[61] The Pantheon also has an unusual northerly orientation.[62] Hannah and Magli have presented compelling evidence that the dome took into account the play of sunlight with the sun's beam shining into the doorway on 21 April, Rome's foundation date, creating the opportunity for an imperial epiphany.[63]

Also in the Campus Martius, Hadrian restored the precinct of the Ara Pacis, which had been inundated by water. He effectively enshrined it in an enclosure. This structure has a relatively unexplored connection to Hadrian's Temple of Venus and Roma (fig. 4). As scholars have noted, Hadrian's idea for the Temple of Venus and Roma was a significant part of initiating a new golden age.[64] In founding the first Roma temple in the city, Hadrian emphasized the security and durability of the state with Roma's epithet "Aeterna." Roma was also closely linked to emperor (fig. 5).[65] Venus was the divine ancestress of Augustus. Nearby, Venus occupied the prominent Julian temple and was part of the cult assemblage in the Augustan Mars Ultor Temple.[66] Her aspect at Hadrian's temple was "Felix."[67] "Felix" had the advantage of not being subject to change or reversal. This moniker harmonized well with Roma's epithet: "Aeterna."[68] These goddesses together already appeared in Republican coinage and on the side of the Ara Pacis that faced the well-travelled Via Flaminia.[69] Here they complemented one another as representatives of Rome's enduring prosperity and security under Augustus.

Hadrian chose a prime location for the Temple of Venus and Roma that the Flavians coopted when they completed Nero's Colossus without his features. Hadrian used the spectacle of 24 elephants to move the Colossus[70] closer to the Colosseum and intended to complement Sol with Luna, a further reference to eternity.[71] Brick stamps in the temple's massive substructure confirm a start date in the 120s.[72]

Running parallel to the Via Sacra, rather than facing it, a peripteral design made sense. Passersby would never be looking at the "back" of the temple. This siting also made the back-to-back cellae advantageous. A goddess peered out whether approached from east or west. The dipteral design and back-to-back cellae also likely alluded to eastern temples for imperial cult, such as the Olympieion and the Temple of Artemis at Sardis.[73]

Hadrian used the memory of Augustus to invigorate present and future.[74] Proclaiming a new Golden Age, bringing the worship of Roma into the city, and converting the Parilia to Romaia were part of a grand vision. Roma was more than a city goddess; she was a stand-in for imperial cult and eternal power.[75] Venus, too, spoke to the divine heritage of the ruler. The goddesses linked Augustus and the history of Rome with Hadrian as the realization of a legacy. The "Greekness" of the new temple and its colossal images resonated with other sites of imperial cult throughout the empire. With this temple, Hadrian could project his current power and predict his eventual deification as Augustus had done before.

Notes

[1] Suet. *Aug.* 7.1; Birley 1997, 96.

[2] Opper 2008, 126: aureus, Roman mint, *RIC* 2 136, 121 C.E.; Birley 1997, 112.

[3] Birley 1997, 16; Boatwright 1987, 72–73.

[4] Boatwright 1987, 51, 71–73; Beaujeu 1955, 126–27: Hadrian as "nouvel Auguste." Zanker (1997, 72–86) noted how acts of the

emperor penetrated everyday life with monuments as regular reminders.

[5] Suet. *Aug.* 52. Also Dio Cass. 51.20. See Gradel (2002, 73–84) on epigraphical evidence for municipal and private worship of Augustus in Italy during his lifetime.

[6] Fishwick 2014, 52: "In Spain alone municipal temples to Augustus already existed in the emperor's lifetime at Carthago Nova, Barcino, Augusta Emerita, and Ebora." Burrell 2004, 3.

[0] *FGH* 90 F 125.

[8] Price 1980, 31.

[9] Suet. *Aug.* 52. Price 1980, 34: "little weight should be given to the traditional argument that Augustus was not worshipped in Italy in his own lifetime."

[10] Hänlein-Schäfer 1985, 16. See Price (1984b, 58) on Augustus having had, at minimum, priests in 34 different cities.

[11] Benjamin 1963, 57; Price 1984b, 216. Price 1980, 34: Hadrian had more altars, but Augustus and "Sebastoi" were in second and third respectively.

[12] Benjamin 1963, 57; Raja 2012, 121–22. Benjamin and Raubitschek 1959, 65–66 noted that one altar to Augustus transformed into one for Tiberius and then for Hadrian; another went from Augustus to Hadrian.

[13] Boatwright 2000, 136. She identified eleven sites. Cahill and Greenewalt 2016, 501: the twelfth would be Sardis.

[14] Birley 1997, 113; *Hist. Aug.* Hadrian 10.1.

[15] Rutherford 2016, 130. Boatwright (2000) 12; see also 127: "Hadrian was involved in building, restoring, or completing twenty temples and shrines in eighteen cities, adding sculpture and architectural decoration to four other shrines in four cities, and working on seven tombs in six different locales." Trajan put greater efforts into roads and harbors, while Hadrian contributed more to religious structures.

[16] Price 1984b, 163.

[17] Tacitus. *Annales* 4.56.

[18] *RIC* 1 230; *Cohen* 209; *RIC* 1 231a; *RCV* 1691.

[19] Fishwick 1972, 50.

[20] Fishwick 2002a, 199. Fishwick 1972, 47: "*Sacerdos ad templum Romae et Augustorum.*" No singular inscriptions are associated with the temple.

[21] Fishwick 1972, 49. Fishwick (2002a, 198) wrote regarding western provinces in the mid-second century: "the majority of provincial cults were largely uniform in worshipping living and dead emperors in combination." And, he noted that Hadrian continued the connection.

[22] Fishwick 1972, 50–51.

[23] *Hist. Aug.* Hadrian 12; Fishwick 1972, 46.

[24] Arrayás Morales 2010, 138–39.

[25] Fishwick 2014, 57–59.

[26] *IGR* IV 39 = *OGIS* 456. Shields (1917, 89) noted numerous inscriptions to Hadrian as divine. On 25, at Eresus, both Augustus and Hadrian had the epithet Olympios.

[27] Tac., *Ann.* 1.78 for 15 C.E. Casas et al. (2009, 277–83) located it under the current cathedral.

[28] Fishwick (2017, 150–58) argued it was provincial temple from its inception.

[29] Mierse 1999, 134: four obverse types, three with Augustus and one with Tiberius as DIVI R. Fishwick 1990, 129: "All other early municipal temples of which the details are known are either hexastyle as at Emerita, Barcino, Evora, Vienne and Ostia, or tetrastyle as a Pola, Carthago Nova and on the Magdalensberg." Here he also compared the octostyle façade to that of Roma and Augustus at Lepcis Magna: Mierse 1999, 137. See also Mierse 1999, 140 on the coins. Woods 1975, 345–54. Fishwick (2014, 52–53) argued that western provinces had little precedent for what temples to divine emperors, living or dead, should look like.

[30] Mierse 1999, 138: "Italic Temple" (*RPC* 224) and "Greek-style Temple" (*RPC* 226).

[31] Mierse 1999, 141.

[32] *RPC* 222 obv.

[33] Birley 1997, 147. *Hist. Aug.* Hadrian 12.3: *aedem Augusti restituit.*

[34] Birley 1997, 148; *ILS* 6930; Fishwick 2002b, 98; 1993, 280.

[35] Birley 1997, 149.

[36] Fraser 2006, 156.

[37] Birley 1997, 147; Syme, 1988, 167.

[38] Birley 1997, 151.

[39] Burrell (2004, 1, 19) observed that the temple became the repository for important documents for the koinon of Asia.

[40] Burrell (2004, 17, 22–30) stated the title "neokoros" did not appear until ca. 100 C.E. Friesen 1993, 10–15.

[41] Dio Cass. 51.20.6–9. The first coins appeared in 19 B.C.E. and showed only the temple (*BMCRE* 705 and 706). Then in 2 B.C.E. (*RPC* 25340) Augustus is alone in a tetrastyle temple; (*RPC* 2369) features Tiberius and Livia on the obverse and Augustius on the reverse in a tetrastyle temple; During the reign of Claudius, (*RIC* 1 120; BMC 228) displays a reverse with a tetrastyle temple inscribed ROMETAVG and Roma crowning Augustus; Nerva (*RIC* 2 123) has a similar reverse to the Claudian coin; Vespasian (*RPC* 2 859/1; RE2 p94.449) again has a similar reverse. See Burrell (2004, 19–20) for a discussion of the coins.

[42] See Friesen (2011, 32–34) on Asia instituting a new calendar that began time with Augustus's birth.

[43] Burrell 2004, 20.

[44] Burrell 2004, 23.

[45] Burrell 2004, 23. See her note 55 on sources regarding correspondence.

[46] Burrell (2004, 22–24) observed that *hymnodoi* singing the praises of Augustus are attested through the Antonine period (*IGRR* 4:460).

[47] Pergamon, bronze, second Neokorate, ca. 113/114, *BMC* 263–265. Burrell (2004, 24–25) also noted that, based on ornament, several scholars have suggested the architect of this temple was the architect of the Temple of Venus and Roma. See her note 73 for references.

[48] Antikensammlung Berlin, AvP VII 281 (Trajan) and AvP VII 282 (Hadrian). According to Burrell (2004, 26–28), the inscription is dated after 135. The figures would be 4.8 m tall. She noted the head of Hadrian resembles the type established in 128. See Burrell's note 88. The addition of the eastern and western porticos likely date to Hadrian's possible visits in either 124 or 129.

[49] Thakur 2008, 108. Augustus likely visited Athens in 22 or 21 B.C.E. See *IG* II2 3173 for a dedicatory inscription. Spawforth (1997, 183–84) observed that the dedication came during a time of unrest.

[50] Thankur 2008, 112–17. The position and alignment of the temple are important. It was placed into the "ancestral pantheon of Athens." However, at only 10 m tall, it could not be seen from the city below. Hurwitt (1999, 275) observed that neither Augustus nor Hadrian sponsored new monuments on the Acropolis.

[51] Boatwright 2000, 144; Rutherford 2016, 129.

[52] Rutherford 2016, 150.

[53] Including Augustus's funding of the Roman Agora (*IG* II2 3175) as well as restorations of monuments; Boatwright 2000, 144–57. Many date to Hadrian's third and final visit.

[54] Suet. *Aug.* 60. Wycherley (1964, 172) argued that Hadrian completed the western end and that a small section on the south side was likely Augustan.

[55] Boatwright 2000, 130. Paus. 1.18.6 on the chryselephantine statue. See also Lapatin (2001, 110), who observed that the Olympian Zeus in Athens was larger than both the colossi of Phidias. Pausanias believed it was larger than all colossi except Rhodes and Rome. Price (1984a, 86) observed the close association between Zeus and Hadrian due to Hadrian's completion of the temple in Athens.

[56] Paus. 1.1.18 noted visitors should see it because it outdid other statues; Benjamin 1963, 58–59; Højte 2000, 232.

[57] Romeo 2002, 21–40. Hadrian dedicated this dipteral temple in 132 when he took title "Panhellenios" and established Panhellenion, an association of ethnically Greek cities. Boatwright (2000, 138) observed that at Smyrna, Cyzicus, and other sites, Hadrian linked himself with Jupiter and emperor worship.

[58] Spawforth and Walker 1985, 94; Boatwright 2000, 150; Raja 2012, 121.

[59] Hetland (2015, 79–98) proposed a Trajanic datie based on

brick stamps and the fact that the fire occurred in 110, allowing sufficient time to work on the project before Trajan died: Trajanic brick stamps date to 114–116. Trajan was away from Rome from 113 until his death in 117, so he never made use of the space.

[60] Dio Cass. 53.27.3; La Rocca 2015, 49, 75. See note 82 for further references.

[61] La Rocca 2015, 52, 63, 66–67. The Hadrianic footprint largely preserved proportions of an earlier round structure, possibly with a wooden roof and oculus.

[62] La Rocca (2015, 60–61) observed that excavations in 1996 and 1997 revealed that the Augustan-period structure also had this orientation, although the Augustan façade was wider and likely decastyle. La Rocca argued against significant Domitianic rebuilding after the fire of 80 C.E. No evidence of fire or a second layer of construction over the Augustan level has been detected. Hannah and Magli (2011, 497) observed that no direct natural light enters the interior from the doorway.

[63] La Rocca 2015, 69. Price (1980, 32) referred to language of accession: "the emperor was a new sun that had risen." Hannah and Magli (2011, 502): April was also the month of Venus.

[64] Boatwright 1987, 130–32. Opper 2008, 126: Aureus, Roman mint, *RIC* 2 136, 121 C.E.

[65] BM R1874,0715.38; *RIC* 2 263A.

[66] Ruck (2007, 54) suggested these three images celebrated gens of Augustus and protective deities, a type of substitution for "Kaiserkulttempel."

[67] Rives 1994, 298.

[68] Pratt 1965, 28.

[69] Galinsky 1969, 234: "The juxtaposition of Venus and Roma is not accidental either. It reached its culmination in the hadrianic temple of Venus and Roma, but is found first on the reverse of the coins of E. Egnatius Maximus in ca. 73 B.C.E. Roma symbolizing the Romulean tradition as she stands on the head of the wolf-nurse, while Venus alludes to the Trojan heritage."

[70] *Hist. Aug.* Hadrian 19.12. According to Albertson (2001, 99–114), the Colossus was not completed by the death of Nero.: "Zenodorus's innovative blend of solar and ruler iconography elevated the meaning of the Colossus to a universal theme of *aeternitas*." Helios/Sol usually had a globe and radiate crown. In his hand were a whip, scepter, globe, torch, and victoria. Here he has a rudder associated with Fortuna and tyches. Elephants were also linked with eternity.

[71] *Hist. Aug.* Hadrian 19.12–16.

[72] Opper 2008, 126. Interestingly, this elevation was among Apollodorus's suggestions for Hadrian in Dio Cassius's recorded critique.

[73] Cahill and Greenewalt 2016, 473–509.

[74] Boatwright 2000, 209.

[75] Joyce 2014, 37–49.

References

Albertson, F. 2001. "Zenodorus's 'Colossus of Nero.'" *MAAR* 46:95–118.

Arrayás Morales, I. 2010. "Diplomacy in the Greek Poleis of Asia Minor." *ClMed* 61:127–49.

Beaujeu, Jean. 1955. *La religion romaine à l'apogée de l'empire.* Paris: Les Belles-Lettres.

Benjamin, A. 1963. "Altars of Hadrian in Athens and Hadrian's Panhellenic Program." *Hesperia* 32:57–86.

Benjamin, A., and A.E. Raubitschek. 1959. "Arae Augusti." *Hesperia* 28:65–85.

Birley, A. 1997. *Hadrian the Restless Emperor.* London: Routledge.

Boatwright, M.T. 1987. *Hadrian and the City of Rome.* Princeton: Princeton University Press.

———. 2000. *Hadrian and the Cities of the Roman Empire.* Princeton: Princeton University Press.

Burrell, B. 2004. *Neokoroi: Greek Cities and Roman Emperors.* Leiden: Brill.

Cahill, N., and C.H. Greenewalt, Jr. 2016. "The Sanctuary of Artemis at Sardis: Preliminary Report, 2002–2102." *AJA* 120:473–509.

Casas, A., P.I. Cosentino, Y. Diaz, et al. 2009. "Integrated Archaeological and Geophysical Survey for Searching the Roman Temple of Augustus in Terragona, Spain." *Quaderni di Palazzo Montablo* 15:277–83.

Fishwick, D. 1972. "The Temple of the Three Gauls." *JRS* 62:46–52.

———. 1990. *The Imperial Cult in the Latin West.* Vol. 1, 1. Leiden: Brill.

———. 1993. *The Imperial Cult in the Latin West.* Vol 1, 2. Leiden: Brill.

———. 2002a. *The Imperial Cult in the Latin West.* Vol. 3, *Provincial Cult.* Part 1: *Institution and Evolution.* Leiden: Brill.

———. 2002b. *The Imperial Cult in the Latin West.* Vol. 3, *Provincial Cult.* Part 2: *The Provincial Priesthood.* Leiden: Brill.

———. 2014. "Augustus and the Cult of the Emperor." *Studia Historica. Historia Antigua* 32:47–60.

———. 2017. *Precinct, Temple and Altar in Roman Spain: Studies on the Imperial Monuments at Mérida and Tarragon.* New York: Routledge.

Fraser, T.E. 2006. *Hadrian as Builder and Benefactor in the Western Provinces.* BAR-IS 1484. Oxford: Archaeopress.

Friesen, S.J. 1993. *Twice Neokoros: Ephesus, Asia and the Cult of the Flavian Imperial Family.* Leiden: Brill.

———. 2011. *Imperial Cults and the Apocalypse of John: Reading Revelation in the Ruins.* Oxford: Oxford University Press.

Galinsky, K. 1969. *Aeneas, Sicily, and Rome.* Princeton: Princeton University Press.

Gradel, I. 2002. *Emperor and Roman Religion.* Oxford: Clarendon Press.

Hänlein-Schäfer, H. 1985. *Veneratio Augusti. Eine Studie zu den Tempeln des ersten römischen Kaisers.* Rome: Bretschneider.

Hannah, R., and G. Magli. 2011. "The Role of the Sun in the Pantheon's Design and Meaning." *Numen* 58:486–513.

Hetland, L. 2015. "New Perspectives on Dating the Pantheon." In *The Pantheon from Antiquity to the Present,* edited by T.A. Marder and M. Wilson Jones, 79–98. Cambridge: Cambridge University Press.

Højte, J.M. 2000. "Imperial Visits as Occasion for the Erection of Portrait Statues?" *ZPE* 133:221–35.

Hurwitt, J. 1999. *The Athenian Acropolis.* Cambridge: Cambridge University Press.

Joyce, L. 2014. "Roma and the Virtuous Breast." *MAAR* 59:1–49.

Lapatin, K. 2001. *Chryselephantine Statuary in the Ancient Mediterranean World.* Oxford: Oxford University Press.

La Rocca, E. 2015. "Agrippa's Pantheon and Its Origins." In *The Pantheon from Antiquity to the Present,* edited by T.A. Marder and M. Wilson Jones, 49–78. Cambridge: Cambridge University Press.

Mierse, W.E. 1999. *Temples and Towns in Roman Iberia: The Social and Architectural Dynamics of Sanctuary Designs, from the Third Century B.C. to the Third Century A.D.* Berkeley: University of California Press.

Opper, T. 2008. *Hadrian Empire and Conflict.* London: Trustees of the British Museum.

Pratt, K. 1965. "Rome as Eternal." *Journal of the History of Ideas* 26:25–44.

Price, S. 1980. "Between Man and God: Sacrifice in the Roman Imperial Cult." *JRS* 70:28–43.

———. 1984a. "Gods and Emperors: The Greek Language of the Roman Imperial Cult." *JHS* 104:79–95.

———. 1984b. *Rituals and Power: The Roman Imperial Cult in Asia Minor.* Cambridge: Cambridge University Press.

Raja, R. 2012. *Urban Development and Regional Identity in the Eastern Roman Provinces, 50 BC—AD 250. Aphrodisias, Ephesos, Athens, Gersa.* Copenhagen: Museum Tusculanum Press.

Rives, J. 1994. "Venus Genetrix outside Rome." *Phoenix* 48:294–306.

Romeo, I. 2002. "The Panhellion and Ethnic Identity in Hadrianic Greece." *CP* 97:21–40.

Ruck, B. 2007. *Die Grossen dieser Welt: Kolossalporträits im antiken Rom.* Heidelberg: Verlag Archäologie und Geschichte.

Rutherford, W. 2016. "Literature: The Politics of Patronage in Hadrianic Athens." In *Stones, Bones, and the Sacred: Essays on Material Culture and Ancient Religion in Honor of Dennis*

E. Smith, edited by A.H. Cadwallader, 129–55. Early Christianity and Its Literature 21. Atlanta: SBL Press.

Shields, E.L. 1917. "The Cults of Lesbos." Ph.D. diss., The Johns Hopkins University.

Spawforth, A.J.S. 1997. "The Early Reception of the Imperial Cults in Athens: Problems and Ambiguities." In *The Romanization of Athens*, edited by M. Hoff and S. Rotroff, 183–201. Oxford: Oxbow.

Spawforth, A.J.S. and S. Walker. 1985. "The World of the Panhellion." *JRS* 75:78–104.

Syme, R. 1988. "Journeys of Hadrian." *ZPE* 73:159–70.

Thakur, S. 2008. "Identity under Construction in Roman Athens." In *Negotiating the Past in the Past: Identity, Memory, and Landscape in Archaeological Research*, edited by N. Yoffee, 104–27. Tucson: University of Arizona Press.

Woods, D.E. 1975. "The Temple of Augustus—Tarragona." In *Classica et Iberica: A Festschrift in Honor of the Reverend Joseph M.-F. Marique, S.J.*, edited by P.T. Brannan, 345–54. Worcester, MA: Institute for Early Christian Iberian Studies.

Wycherley, R.E. 1964. "The Olympieion at Athens." *GRBS* 5:161–79.

Zanker, P. 1997. "The Power of Images." In *Paul and Empire: Power in Roman Imperial Society*, edited by R. Horsley, 72–86. Harrisburg, PA: Trinity Press International.

Sabina's "Plotina" Portrait Type

Fae Amiro

Abstract

The sequence and dating of the empress Sabina's portrait types has been debated for the past ninety years. By far her most common type on coinage is the so-called Plotina type. Most scholars believe that this portrait type was meant to form a visual connection between Sabina and her predecessor, Plotina. However, there are several problems with this assumption. Most importantly, comparison between the two shows that their similarities have been exaggerated and that they bear almost no resemblance in their details.

I conducted die studies of Sabina's aurei and dupondii/asses to determine the chronology of Sabina's coinage and contextualize the Plotina type. The die sequencing places the start of the type around the third year of minting, ca. 130/131 C.E., which corresponds with evidence from Egypt, where the type debuts around the same year. At this time, Hadrian and Sabina were abroad, which raises questions about the mechanisms of portrait type creation. I argue that this portrait type was not meant to represent continuity with the previous dynasty, but is a departure from it, as seen in the change from the old Matidia portrait type to one that is stylistically distinct from those of the previous dynasty.

THE EMPRESS SABINA'S COIN PORTRAITURE SET A NEW precedent for the representation of Roman empresses. It is both wider in variety and larger in quantity than that of her predecessors, and these changes were followed by her successors.[1] On her coinage, Sabina has five portrait types, all produced between the years 128 and 138 C.E.[2] In previous scholarship, these types have been given both a relative chronology and standard interpretation. Sabina's first two portrait types, nicknamed the "turban" (fig. 1) and the "Plotina" (fig. 2) by Carandini, have been interpreted as Trajanic in style, imitating the coiffures of Matidia and Plotina, respectively.[3] Her third type is believed to have been made to commemorate her initiation into the Eleusinian mysteries, and has therefore been named the Eleusis type.[4] The fourth, more recently distinguished type, is seen as an allusion to classical goddess

Fig. 1. The obverse of an aureus showing Sabina's earliest coin portrait type, the turban (courtesy of the American Numismatic Society, ANS 1967.153.145).

imagery and is called the "Aphrodite."[5] Her final type is post-humous and shows the empress veiled.

Sabina's most common coin portrait type is the Plotina type, which is found on over half of all coins minted in her name at the Roman mint. Despite its ubiquity on coinage, the type has received little scholarly attention. This stems from its rarity in sculpted replicas. Fittschen only identifies three replicas of the type in the round.[6] Carandini, in his 1969 monograph on the portraits of Sabina, called this type's hairstyle "alla Plotina" and characterized it as a "western" hair-style.[7] He believed that there were strong parallels between this and Plotina's main type, even going so far as to state that Sabina never actually wore this hairstyle, but that instead it was used as a demonstration of dynastic continuity between Hadrian and Trajan.[8] Fittschen and Zanker have a similar opinion and connect it with Hadrian's attempt to regain le-gitimacy through his coinage ca. 128.[9] Recently, the standard interpretation of the hairstyle has been questioned by Abdy , Stephens, and Brennan.[10]

The association by previous scholars between this Sabina type and Plotina's main portrait type is based mostly on the fact that both hairstyles are queues.[11] A number of details, however, show that there are major typological distinctions between the two. Both have long hair hanging at the back of the head and a crest of hair at the front, but Plotina's hair is

Fig. 2. The obverse of an aureus showing Sabina's Plotina portrait type (courtesy of the American Numismatic Society, ANS 1944.100.45592).

braided through the entire back and is looped into one long ring which is fastened at the nape of the neck (fig. 3). Sabina's hair is not braided in the back and is fastened at the end of the hair. The front of Plotina's hair has a coiled row of locks along the brow, similar to Sabina's first portrait type, and there is a diadem behind the crest of hair. Sabina's hair has no row of locks in the front and no diadem. She instead appears with either a crown of wheat or fillet around her head. Stylistically, Sabina's queue hairstyle does not fit in with the rigid, austere Trajanic style. Unlike in her first portrait type, Sabina's hair here appears loose and free flowing, with little adornment, braiding, or styling compared to both her own earlier portrait types and those of the women of the previous reign.

If not a reference to Plotina, what was the intent behind the creation of this portrait type? To answer this, the questions of when and where it was made need to be addressed. I conducted two die studies, on the *aurei* and *dupondii/asses* from the Roman imperial mint, the results of which are helpful in answering these questions. Their answers pose new questions concerning the mechanisms of portrait type creation when the emperor was outside of Rome. The evidence provided by the coins suggests that, instead of referring back to images of the previous reign, the queue portrait type is

Fig. 3. The obverse of an aureus showing Plotina's only coin portrait type (courtesy of the American Numismatic Society, ANS 1967.153.139).

instead the first move in Sabina's coinage towards the new, Hadrianic portrait style.

The Die Study

Neither numismatists nor portrait scholars have reached a consensus on the relative sequence and exact dating for the introduction of this type or Sabina's portrait types in general.[12] I conducted die studies of Sabina's *aurei* and *dupondii/asses* to determine the relative chronological sequence of Sabina's coin types from the Roman imperial mint.

Die studies are a way to recreate a given coin production chronology through the analysis of the extant coins. Ancient coins were made by striking two stamps, that is, dies, onto a blank piece of metal. Through intensive use, these dies would inevitably break or wear out, requiring them to be replaced. Since these dies were hand-carved, even if the content of the image remained the same, there were still observable differences between the new and old dies. Usually both dies were not replaced at the same time, which resulted in two groups of coins being produced that shared the same die on one face but not the other. By careful analysis of a large enough body of coinage, a chain of linked coins can be created that forms an objective relative chronology. Unfortunately, there are sometimes breaks in the chain where either coins from a die pair do not survive or both dies were replaced at the same time, possibly after the introduction of a new design. The order of these groups can be determined by the sequence of inscription and reverse types.

I assembled a database of 202 unique *aurei* issued in Sabina's name by the Roman imperial mint which, after die analysis, proved to have been struck from 23 obverse dies and 28 reverse dies. The die study produced a sequence of *aurei* in which both obverse inscription and portrait type have no chronological overlap. Twelve of the 23 obverse dies (52%) have Sabina's queue portrait type on them. I similarly analyzed 225 *dupondii/asses*, which were assessed to have been struck from 106 obverse and 139 reverse dies. The queue is found on 52 of the 106 obverse dies (49%). I did not conduct a die study of Sabina's *denarii* or *sestertii*, but the catalogues of the British Museum and ANS show similarly high percentages of coins with the queue hairstyle in these denominations.[13]

In the die sequence of Roman imperial *aurei*, the queue comes second, after the so-called turban type. There is no die link between these two groups, but this order is confirmed by the sequence of obverse inscriptions, since one inscription overlaps between the two groups. The queue type remains in use through one change in obverse inscription, from the longer SABINA AVGVSTA HADRIANI AVG PP to simply SABINA AVGVSTA. The queue's use on *aurei* ends with the introduction of the Aphrodite type. The Eleusis type is not used on this denomination.

The *dupondii/asses* present a more complicated picture. Like the *aurei*, the first type used with these coins is the turban, but it is not immediately followed by the queue on all of the coins. On the *asses*, the Eleusis type intervenes between the turban and the queue. The *dupondii* do not feature the Eleusis type. This conclusion is based on weight and die-link analysis. In antiquity, *dupondii* and *asses* would have been differentiable by color and weight, but the extant coins are too discolored to use the former. Hadrian's *dupondii* pre-128 were further distinguished by the use of a radiate crown on the obverse portrait, which the *asses* lacked. Therefore, a comparison of the weights of a group of Sabina's coins with the known weights of pre-128 Hadrian *dupondii* and *asses* can help determine to which denomination those Sabina coins belong.[14] Sabina's Eleusis portrait type coins have a median weight of 10.62 grams, while those with the queue portrait type (divided into two groups based on the different obverse inscription types) have median weights of 11.68 and 11.60 grams. Hadrian's pre-128 coins have median weights of 12.61 for *dupondii* and 10.95 for *asses*. The Eleusis type most likely appears on only *asses*, while the queue appears on both *asses* and *dupondii*. The Eleusis type appears on only 13 of the 106 obverse dies. There is a die link between one Eleusis type die and a queue type die. It therefore appears that the type was used on *asses* for a brief period, while the *dupondii* were minted with the turban or the queue. After the run of the Eleusis type finished on the *asses*, they were minted with the queue. As with the *aurei*, the queue appears on *dupondii/asses* with two obverse inscriptions and continues in use until the introduction of the Aphrodite type.

Dating the Queue and Sabina's Location during the Type's Use

The die-study results can be used to date the introduction and conclusion of the use of the queue on Sabina's coinage. There are, unfortunately, no topical references on the reverses of this coinage from which specific dates can be argued. However, the die studies have provided a relative chronology of the types. If it can be assumed that there were similar numbers of coins minted each year, estimates for the introduction and conclusion of the use of the type can be made. There are problems with this method, since not enough is known about the yearly workings of the mint to be sure that it had such a consistent output. These estimates can, however, be useful in conjunction with other evidence for providing approximate years around which the type was most likely used.

Knowing that Sabina's coinage begins in 128 and ends in 138, there would be around two obverse dies struck each year for the *aurei*. This would give a date of around the year 130/131 for the introduction of the queue type. For the *dupondii/asses*, if the Eleusis type's use for the *asses* is assumed to overlap with another type on the *dupondii*, the introduction of the queue would date to 131/132. Both *aurei* and *dupondii/asses* would have used the type for approximately five years, ending somewhere in the years 135–137.

Fortunately, there is additional evidence for the queue's introduction date. The best evidence comes from coinage from

Alexandria that uses a similar hairstyle (fig. 4). Coins from Alexandria had their year of minting written on them. The Alexandrian queue portrait type first appears in the Alexandrian year 15, which is equivalent to the year 130/131 C.E. Evidence of the Emperor's travels places Hadrian's traveling group in Egypt from July/August of 130 until early 131.[15] Sabina's presence on this journey is attested by the epigrams of Julia Balbilla, which state that the poet was "σὺν τῇ Σεβαστῇ Σαβεινηι" (with Sabina Augusta) at the colossi of Memnon in November of 130.[16] The empress only appears with her hair down for the years 15 and 16, or 130/131 C.E. and 131/132 C.E., the time during which she was present in Egypt.[17]

Given the similarity between this Alexandrian portrait type and the Roman queue type and given the presence of the empress in Egypt during its likely time of introduction, the type must have been introduced in both places around the same time. This conclusion is supported by the die estimates, which give a date similar to the Alexandrian one. This also correlates with the known close connection between the Alexandrian and imperial mints.[18]

There is also provincial coinage that helps determine the end date for the queue's use. Assuming that the die estimates are at least close to correct, the next type must have been introduced sometime after the imperial couple's return to Rome in the first quarter of 133 and before Sabina's own death in early 138.[19] Sabina's next portrait type, the Aphrodite, appears on coinage from Amisus in 135/6.[20] Since the couple had already been in Rome for several years before the type's introduction on provincial coinage, the type must have been invented at Rome. It therefore must have been introduced at the capital before Amisus, necessitating its introduction in Rome in 135/6. There are too few coins with the Aphrodite type for an earlier date to be likely. The end of the use of the queue must date to the same year, 135/6.

Sabina's Travels and the Mechanisms of Portrait Type Creation

Based on the dating, the queue must have been introduced while Sabina was abroad. There are two possible ways to explain how the type came into use: it was either created in Alexandria while Sabina was there in person or in Rome while she was abroad. Both of these explanations are problematic for the standard understanding of how portrait types were usually produced.

The two main theories about type creation are those proposed by Fittschen and Fejfer. According to Fittschen's theory, a new portrait type would be centrally commissioned for an imperial workshop. A model of it would then be produced in Rome out of either clay or marble, or on parchment, which would be given to the mint and sent through the empire for copying.[21] In Fejfer's view, imperial portrait types were not centrally commissioned, but instead created through competition between independent workshops within Rome.[22] According to this theory, the court was still invested in the appearance of the types and approval by the imperial court was still required before the adoption of the portrait type for official use.[23]

Neither theory necessitates the presence of the portrait's subject for the creation of the new type. If the type were to reflect the realities of the person's appearance, a version of it must have been created with the subject present. This is, of course, not a necessary condition for a portrait type change. However, the queue is a hairstyle that is unique to Sabina in its details and the type is a departure from her previous coin portrait type in not only coiffure but also physiognomy. If the type was invented at Rome, it means that a drastically different, new portrait type was invented without the emperor, empress, or many important court officials present. This seems highly unlikely.

The other, more probable possibility is that the new type was invented in Egypt in the presence of the empress. If so, there are several ways in which it could have been introduced to the Roman mint. It is possible that only a sketch or model of the type was invented in Egypt before being sent to the capital for reproduction by the imperial mint, and copies of this model were then sent throughout the empire via the normal channels from Rome. It is also, however, possible that not only was the type invented in Egypt, but its first appearance in public was on the Alexandrian coins.[24] Those who usually oversaw the creation of official portrait types could have been present on the trip already, or Hadrian could have used his authority to break from usual practices in this instance.

It seems most likely that the type was invented in Egypt at the behest of the court and was planned for use by the Roman mint from the beginning.[25] Otherwise, one might expect evidence of a gap in time between the type's introduction in Egypt and in Rome. After its creation, the type was also used locally by the Alexandrian mint and made to suit Egyptian tastes. Which mint produced the first coins with this image is impossible to say. The minting in the two cities can be said to be roughly contemporaneous and both were planned uses of the original model from its inception. This conclusion is compatible with both Fittschen and Fejfer's theories, although it assumes that the practices they describe occurring in Rome were able to be moved along with the court on Hadrian's travels.

The Queue and Imperial Messaging

All but one of the major works on Sabina's coin portraiture note the similarities between the queue hairstyle and that of Plotina.[26] This similarity, according to the theory, was meant to promote Hadrian's legitimacy by referring to the previous dynasty. This message of dynastic continuity was already done more clearly in Sabina's first, turban portrait type, which really was an almost direct copy of Matidia's hairstyle (fig. 5).[27]

The queue and Plotina's hairstyle also have less in common than previously stated. This becomes even more apparent when the hairstyles are compared with images of previous empresses. Queue hairstyles are found on several empresses' coinage before Plotina, including Agrippina Maior, Agrip-

Fig. 5. The obverse of an aureus showing Matidia's only coin portrait type (courtesy of the American Numismatic Society, ANS 1967.153.180).

pina Minor, Domitilla, Julia Titi, and Domitia.[28] All of these women's queues are braided and fastened at the nape, like Plotina's. None display the hair's natural texture in the queue and none are fastened at the end of the hair, as Sabina's is. The Sabina style of queue is absent from earlier Roman imperial portraiture.

There are, however, parallels for the hairstyle found in Greek art. Athenian coins and a sculpture from Tusculum, both from Hadrian's reign, show Athena with a queue fastened at the end, although she wears a helmet that masks the front of her hair (fig. 6).[29] This queue is braided in the fishtail style, unlike Sabina's, which is left loose. Similar queues can be seen on the Caryatids of the Erechtheion in Athens.[30] The Roman copy of a Greek original statue of Artemis/ Diana has a queue of loose hair attached at the bottom.[31] The statue wears a fillet like the one Sabina wears, but the front lacks the crest of hair characteristic of the Sabina style. While Sabina's coiffure is still unique, these examples bear more similarity to Sabina's hairstyle than those of imperial women. This could be an indication that Greek goddess imagery was an important influence on Sabina's queue portrait type's development.[32] This is bolstered by Sabina's appearance on the Alexandrian coins. The version from Egypt likens the

Empress to Demeter-Isis through the presence of a poppy on her headdress.[33] Additionally, some of the imperial coins show Sabina wearing a wheat wreath instead of a fillet, which may be an allusion to goddess imagery, in particular fertility goddesses like Ceres and Demeter.[34]

If, however, the type had a strong association with fertility cults in the Roman context, it was not emphasized, especially on the reverses of the coins. Of the six reverse types found with this portrait type, all of which are female goddesses and personifications, none represent Ceres/Demeter or make reference to the realm of Isis.[35] It seems that while the queue may have been aesthetically inspired by divine imagery, there was not a strong effort by the imperial mint to preserve the religious impact of the statement.

The queue therefore seems best summed up as a Hellenizing type, much like the portrait type that follows it, the Aphrodite. Understanding the queue in this way creates a new picture of the mode of representation for the Empress. Instead of a dynastically connotated stylistic choice, making reference to Plotina, a woman who was famously conservative in her own self-representation, the type may be quite the opposite. The change to a uniquely Hadrianic style no longer seems to have happened only at the very end of Sabina's life, with the introduction of the Aphrodite type following the couple's final return from abroad. Instead, this change appears not only to have happened much sooner, but in much greater abundance than has been previously acknowledged. This also potentially disrupts the standard understanding of Sabina's role in the messaging of Hadrian's administration. By the time of the introduction of the queue, her public image was no longer used solely as a vehicle for promoting Hadrian's legitimacy through her familial connections. The queue portrait type instead modified Sabina's public image to represent the new, distinctly Hadrianic style.

Notes

[1] For example, Duncan-Jones (2006, 224, n. 5) estimates that women accounted for 2 percent of gold coinage and less of silver and bronze under Trajan, while Sabina's coinage was estimated at 16 percent of gold, 14 percent of silver, and 7 percent of bronze coinage.

[2] Works previous to Abdy (2014) described four portrait types, since the turban and Aphrodite were conflated as one type. Abdy's forthcoming new edition of *RIC* 2 subdivides Sabina's coin imagery into seven types based on differences of headdress. See Brennan (2018, appendix 1) for these divisions. For the purposes of this work, I have kept the typology to the five main types, accepting changes in headdress as variants of the same type as opposed to distinct types.

[3] Mattingly and Sydenham 1926, 318; Strack 1933, 23; Mattingly 1936, cxviii; Carandini 1969, 104–6; Nicolai 2007, 94; Brennan 2018, 91–92.

[4] Strack 1933, 23; Carandini 1969, 106; Nicolai 2007, 95.

[5] Adembri 2007, 79; Abdy 2014; Brennan 2018, 91, 170.

[6] Fittschen and Zanker 1983, 10.

[7] Carandini 1969, 237.

[8] Carandini 1969, 106.

[9] Fittschen and Zanker 1983, 10.

[10] Stephens 2017. Abdy (2014, 79) suggests that the type as seen on Egyptian coins is related to the type in Rome. Brennan (2018, 168) echoes Abdy, but elsewhere supports the association between the type and Plotina (91–92, 168, 170).

[11] Mattingly and Sydenham 1926, 318; Strack 1933, 23; Carandini 1966, 106; Nicolai 2007, 94; Adembri 2007, 78; Brennan 2018, 91–92, 170.

[12] It is agreed that Sabina's coinage began in the year 128, or very shortly before, and stopped after Hadrian's death in 138, following a brief period of posthumous minting for the Empress. The date of 128 is confirmed by the presence of PP (Pater Patriae) in Hadrian's titles on all but a very small number of Sabina's earliest coins. It is known from Euseb. *Chron.* Olympiad 226.12 (Helm 1984, 99) and data from military diplomas (Eck 1982, 220–21) that Hadrian

gained that title in 128. Based on the small amount of coins minted for Sabina posthumously, it does not seem likely that minting continued after Hadrian's death.

[13] Sixty-nine percent of *sestertii* and 78 percent of *denarii*.

[14] The pre-128 weight was used because the radiate crown was eliminated from Hadrian's coinage after this year, making distinction between the two denominations as difficult as it is for Sabina's coins. In order to ensure that the weight standard was not changed significantly at this time, I calculated the average weights for Hadrian's *dupondii* and *asses* together both pre- and post-128. The median weight pre-128 was 11.59 and post-128 was 11.41. If there was any alteration, it was likely to make the coins lighter, which corresponds with the lower weight for Sabina's Eleusis type coins.

[15] Halfmann 1986, 194, 207–9.

[16] *CIG* 4730–31.

[17] Abdy 2014, 79. For evidence of the imperial couple's travels during this time, see Halfmann 1986, 193–94, 207–9.

[18] *RPC* III, 544–45.

[19] For a return date of 133, see Eck, Holder, and Pangerl 2010, 195–97. For Sabina's death date, see Nordbø 1988, 174; Hahn 1994, 274; Abdy 2014, 84.

[20] Abdy 2014, 83. For Sabina coins at Amisus, see Nordbø 1988, 166 and *RPC* III, 147–48; 152–53.

[21] Fittschen 1971, 220.

[22] Fejfer 1998, 47; 2008, 416–18.

[23] Fejfer 2008, 418–19.

[24] Abdy 2014, 79.

[25] Abdy (2014, 79) suggests that the type was invented by the Alexandrian mint, which was unaware that the type would be adopted by the imperial mint. While possible, this seems unlikely given the close relationship between the Alexandrian mint and the Roman imperial mint and given the presence of the emperor and his entourage in Alexandria at the time. Also, the type was most likely introduced at Rome while Sabina was still in Egypt, making communication between the two mints from the beginning more likely.

[26] Mattingly and Sydenham 1926, 318; Strack 1933, 23; Mattingly 1936, cxviii; Carandini 1969, 104–6; Nicolai 2007, 94; Brennan 2018, 91–92, 170. Cf. Abdy 2014.

[27] Fittschen's argument that the queue portrait type dates to the year 128 in connection with Hadrian's dynastic-themed coinage is more compatible with the earlier, turban coin portrait type, which started being minted in 128 (Fittschen and Zanker 1983, 10).

[28] For example, *BMCRE* 1, Caligula 7–8, Nero 1–3; *BMCRE* 2, Titus 136–38, 139–43, Domitian 58, 60–67, 503.

[29] Head 1888, nos. 671–816; Vierneisel 1979, 136–46.

[30] I would like to thank F. de Angelis for suggesting the Caryatids as a stylistic parallel for the queue portrait type.

[31] Stephens 2017; Museum of Fine Arts, Houston inv. 74.253.

[32] Stephens 2017.

[33] Abdy 2014, 79; Geissen 2008, 222–23; Hahn 1994, 280–81.

[34] Mikocki 1995, 56.

[35] The reverse types found with the queue portrait type are Concordia Augusta, Juno Regina, Pietas, Pudicitia, Venus Genetrix, and Vesta.

References

Abdy, R.A. 2014. "Chronology of Sabina's Coinage at the Roman Mint." *RN* 171:73–91.

Adembri, B. 2007. "In margine all'iconografia di Sabina." In *Vibia Sabina: da Augusta a Diva*, edited by B. Adembri and R.M. Nicolai, 75–86. Milan: Mondadori Electa.

Amandry, M., and A. Burnett. 2015. *Roman Provincial Coinage*. Vol. 3, *Nerva, Trajan and Hadrian*. London: The British Museum Press.

Brennan, T.C. 2018. *Sabina Augusta: An Imperial Journey*. Cambridge: Cambridge University Press.

Carandini, A. 1969. *Vibia Sabina: Funzione politica, iconografia e il problema del classicismo Adrianeo*. Florence: Leo S. Olschki.

Duncan-Jones, R.P. 2006. "Crispina and the Coinage of the Empresses." *NC* 166:223–28.

Eck, W. 1982. "Hadrian als Pater Patriae und die Verleihung des Augustatitels an Sabina." In *Romanitas-Christianitas, Festschrift J. Straub*, edited by G. Wirth, 217–29. Berlin: Walter de Gruyter.

Eck, W., P. Holder, and A. Pangerl. 2010. "A Diploma for the Army of Britain in 132 and Hadrian's Return to Rome from the East." *ZPE* 174:189–200.

Fejfer, J. 1998. "The Roman Emperor Portrait. Some Problems in Methodology." *Ostraka* 5:45–56.

———. 2008. *Roman Portraits in Context*. Berlin: Walter de Gruyter.

Fittschen, K. 1971. "Zum angeblichen Bildnis des Lucius Verus im Thermen-Museum." *JdI* 86:214–52.

Fittschen, K., and P. Zanker. 1983. *Katalog der römischen Porträts in den Capitolinischen Museen und den anderen kommunalen sammlungen der Stadt Rom*. Vol. 3, *Kaiserinnen- und Prinzessinnenbildnisse Frauenporträts*. Mainz: Philipp von Zabern.

Geissen, A. 2008. "Sabina-Demeter-Isis: Eine Klarstellung." In *Aegyptiaca serta in Soheir Bakhoum memoriam: Mélanges de numismatique, d'iconographie et d'histoire*, edited by D. Gerin, A. Geissen, and M. Amandy, 221–28. Milan: Edizioni Ennerre.

Hahn, U. 1994. *Die Frauen des römischen Kaiserhauses und ihre ehrungen im griechischen Osten anhand epigraphischer und numismatischer Zeugnisse von Livia bis Sabina*. Saarbrücken: Saarbrücker Druckerei und Verlag.

Halfmann, H. 1986. *Itinera principum: Geschicht und Typologie der Kaiserreisen im römischen Reich.* Stuttgart: Franz Steiner.

Head, B.V. 1888. *A Catalogue of the Greek Coins in the British Museum. Attica-Megaris-Aegina.* London; repr. Bologna: Arnaldo Forni, 1963.

Helm, R., ed. 1984. *Eusebius Werke.* Vol. 7, *Die Chronik des Hieronymus.* Berlin: Akademie-Verlag.

Mattingly, H. 1936. *Coins of the Roman Empire in the British Museum.* Vol. 3, *Nerva to Hadrian.* London: The Trustees of the British Museum.

Mattingly, H., and E.A. Sydenham. 1926. *The Roman Imperial Coinage.* Vol. 2, *Vespasian to Hadrian.* London: Spink & Son.

Mikocki, T. 1995. *Sub specie Deae: Les impératrices et princesses romaines assimilées à des déesses. Étude iconologique.* RdA. Suppl. 14. Rome: L'Erma di Bretschneider.

Nicolai, R.M. 2007. "Le monete emesse a nome di Sabina." In *Vibia Sabina: da Augusta a Diva,* edited by B. Adembri and R.M. Nicolai, 87–108. Milan: Mondadori Electa.

Nordbø, J.H. 1988. "The Imperial Silver Coinage of Amisus 131/2– 137/8 A.D." In *Studies in Ancient History and Numismatics Presented to Rudi Thomsen,* edited by A. Damsgaard-Madsen et al., 166–78. Aarhus: Aarhus University Press.

Stephens, J. 2017. "The "Juno" Hairstyle of Empress Sabina." YouTube video, 10:23. https://www.youtube.com/watch?v =74AT70NC9xQ.

Strack, P.L. 1933. *Untersuchungen zur Römischen Reichsprägung des Zweiten Jahrhunderts.* Teil II, *Die Reichsprägung zur Zeit des Hadrian.* Stuttgart: Kohlhammer.

Vierneisel, K., ed. 1979. *Glyptothek München Katalog der Skulpturen.* Vol. 2, *Klassische Skulpturen des 5. und 4. Jahrhunderts v. Chr.* Munich: C. H. Beck.

The Archaeology of Apotheosis: Roman Imperial Funerary Pyres and Commemorative Coinages of the Antonine Dynasty

Steven Burges

Abstract

The aim of this paper is to explicate the critical role of Roman coinage depicting funerary pyres in the imperial cult of the second and third centuries C.E. Images of the ephemeral structures built for imperial cremations asserted dynastic stability and authority in moments of uncertainty and perpetuated the traditional public ritual of divinization. Obverses emblazoned with these temporary constructions ultimately commemorated the genesis of particular imperial devotion at the sites of ustrina and communicated familial piety essential to the propaganda of continuity.

A SHORT TIME AFTER A BAND OF REBELS ACCOMPLISHED the brutal assassination of Gaius Julius Caesar on 15 March 44 B.C.E., a mob of the dictator's supporters seized his corpse during the funeral procession.[1] The horde ultimately burned the body on an impromptu pyre in the heart of the Roman Forum, disrupting staunch cultural tradition and the earliest codified regulations at Rome, which prohibited such intramural mortuary activity.[2] Although his remains were not interred within the Forum, the extraordinary location of Caesar's immolation helped to associate him with the honors no citizen since Romulus had achieved in Rome.[3]

The monument constructed at the Julian *ustrinum* (the physical space of the cremation) also complemented the nearby Lapis Niger complex, an earlier altar with a column associated with the apotheosis of Rome's founder.[4] Suetonius reports that a column and altar were immediately erected adjacent to it, where Julius was burned, and the plebeians treated it like a cult site: "At the foot of this [solid column of

Fig. 1. (A) The core of the circular altar of the Temple of Divus Julius in the Roman Forum still remains within the central hemicycle of the temple's (B) podium with the Temple of Antoninus Pius and Faustina behind it to the southeast (photographs by the author, 2017).

Numidian marble] they continued for a long time to sacrifice, make vows, and settle some of their disputes by an oath in the name of Caesar."[5] These public practices amounted to more than simple tribute to a deceased individual. The people had acclaimed the divinity of Julius Caesar upon his death, probably before the Senate issued the unprecedented decree (the *consecratio*) of his posthumous elevation to the heavenly rank of *divus*.[6]

The disappearance of his corpse and wax image (remarkably reproduced with 23 stab wounds) in the flames of the pyre reproduced the mythical aphanismos of Romulus, and the altar (fig. 1A) of Augustus's temple for Divus Julius would come to stand on the site of the first unofficial *monumentum*.[7] Such commemoration and sustentation at the locus of the ruler's cremation attest to the persistent significance of the destructive public deification at Rome, and the need for fashioning a collective memory of that event drove not only the recurrent dedication of individual *ustrina* memorials but also the inception of novel mementos of the consecration on another type of imperial monument: coinage.

Nearly two centuries after the dedication of the later temple for Caesar (fig. 1B), a new addition to the eastern Forum, the Temple of Antoninus and Faustina, arose in its shadow and established a critical reciprocity with the earlier site of deification and a sense of continuity for the imperial dynasties.[8] In late October of the year 140 C.E., after less than three years of her husband's rule, the empress of Rome, Faustina, died, and the senate declared her posthumous reception into the Roman pantheon, voting to provide the aforementioned temple, priestesses, games, and statues of precious metals for the initiation of a cult devoted to the new goddess.[9] Faustina's consort, Antoninus Pius, lived until 161 C.E., and throughout the intervening 21 years, he ordered an unprecedented series of coins to be struck in her honor, including a sestertius (fig. 2) imprinted with an image of the highly embellished, multistoried funeral pyre on which she was cremated, the first instance of this subject in all of Roman art.[10]

While currency issued in the name of deceased imperial family members was commonplace by the time of Antoninus, Faustina the elder appeared on by far the most diverse and largest set of memorial currency ever minted at Rome. In any given year between 140 and 161 C.E., one-third of the total output of the capital's mint was devoted to the coins of the deified Faustina.[11] The surge in production of these miniature tools of ideological dissemination reflected the continued veneration of various members of the Roman imperial family. Many reverses depicted pyres and other aspects of the *funus* or the commemorative architecture, but some envisioned the *consecratio* as an allegorical ascension on the back of a personification (fig. 3), perhaps referencing the sculptural reliefs decorating *ustrina* monuments like the ascent of Diva Sabina from the Arco di Portogallo.[12] As Alan Shapiro has pointed out, however, the idea that an individual was assumed wholly into heaven during apotheosis precludes the establishment of a traditional hero cult at the burial site of a mortal being.[13] The memory of the short-lived pyres and their locations offered a solution for the ritual needs of the cult of these state ancestors.

Despite their ephemeral nature, individualized funerary pyres would embellish the consecration coins of nearly every deified Roman emperor and empress for the century that followed the death of Faustina the elder, even in the face of a comprehensive shift in second-century numismatic representations towards generic and connotative imagery, such as personifications, and a growing majority of Roman elite who preferred inhumation to cremation.[14] The perseverance of this type throughout the second century and into the third indicates its centrality in what we might call the archaeology of apotheosis, which is a difficult enterprise, since in antiquity this metamorphosis was closely tied to the complete destruction of the material evidence upon the pyre. The coins preserve renderings that each have particular adaptations, but they possess predominant similarities across denomination

Fig. 2. Sestertius of Antoninus
Pius with bust of Diva Faustina
(obverse) and her three-story
funeral pyre (reverse), ca.
140 C.E., D. 35.6 mm, bronze
(Münzkabinett, Kunsthistorisches Museum, Vienna: RÖ
11440; photograph courtesy of
the Münzkabinett, Kunsthistorisches Museum, Vienna).

and type. These artifacts, which traversed social boundaries and reached wide audiences, recognize the topography of the deification process within what Eve D'Ambra has labeled Rome's "fugitive cityscape" and perpetuate an ideology of eternity by representing the static, yet forever-gone, architecture of the pyres without human agents or destructive flames as ambivalent symbols of the process of immortalization.[15]

The unlit pyres symbolized regeneration more than destruction, and earlier coins celebrating imperial divinization featured phoenixes with nimbuses or soaring eagles with the souls of dynasts upon their backs: The process of apotheosis was one of rebirth.[16] This latter motif of dynamic divinization made its debut on Roman currency with the reverses of aurei announcing the consecration of Vibia Sabina, Hadrian's wife, who passed away in 136 or 137.[17] They portray the ascent of the former empress, who holds a scepter, gazes upward, and is framed by a windswept mantle, as she rides on the eagle in the manner of earlier male imperials represented within singular artworks such as the coffered soffit of the arch of Titus and within the mass-produced and widely distributed metallic fittings for legionary armor.[18] It is inscribed, like the previous examples, with the word *consecratio*.

The novel coins minted for empresses bear witness to the incredible importance of the apotheoses of imperial women, who embodied both a tangible connection from the current regime to the revered family of Trajan and a fictive fertility that provided for future dynastic continuity in a period when circumstances of adoption could fall into question.[19] In fact,

Fig. 3. Sestertius of Antoninus Pius with bust of Diva Faustina (obverse) and the deified empress seated atop a winged figure (reverse), ca. 140 C.E., D. 34 mm, bronze (Münzkabinett, Staatliche Museen zu Berlin: AM-011/049; photograph courtesy of the Münzkabinett, Staatliche Museen zu Berlin).

Hadrian had also strengthened his ties to Trajan by elevating several Ulpian women to godhood, including Faustina's great-grandmother and Trajan's beloved sister, Ulpia Marciana, whose image adorned the first imperial coin to be inscribed with *consecratio*, a text accompanied by characteristic aquiline imagery on the reverse.[20]

A similar issue honors the deified Matidia (fig. 4), Marciana's daughter and Hadrian's mother-in-law, and upon her death, Hadrian granted her cult an altar and temple, the first full-scale sanctuary dedicated solely to a Roman woman.[21] Hadrian also detailed, in his funerary oration for her, that she was to be cremated on a monumental pyre and implied that this was a measure of significant distinction.[22] Ancient authors elaborated on the form and spectacular decoration of such funerary constructions, which were adorned with gold and ivory reliefs, wax paintings, gold thread tapestries, and military spoils, before their complete incineration.[23]

Returning to the coin honoring Faustina, it is evident that her pyre stood upon a garlanded podium and consisted of three tiers, each successively smaller than the one below it. Within the first and largest level, six columns supported an entablature, which may have possessed a concave, multisided plan, and a grand doorway surmounted by a tympanum marked the entrance to a chamber that held the corpse. The middle tier seems to have been draped in fabric, while the uppermost story was decorated by a grid pattern, possibly delineating a cage for an eagle, which was released during the event as a symbol of the heaven-bound soul, if scholarly specula-

115

Fig. 4. Aureus of Hadrian with bust of Diva Matidia (obverse) and an eagle perched on a scepter (reverse), ca. 119 C.E., D. 20 mm, gold (Münzkabinett, Staatliche Museen zu Berlin: BM-032/082; photograph courtesy of the Münzkabinett, Staatliche Museen zu Berlin).

tion is to be believed.[24] This ritual embodies a dramatic enactment of the allegorical ascension found on Sabina's coins with these birds (and it causes one to wonder what fate might have befallen the poor feathered creatures should the release mechanism have failed when the structure was ignited.) At the pinnacle of the towering pyre, a statue of the deceased driving a biga appeared in profile.

A coin minted after the divinization of Faustina's daughter portrays the later empress, who was married to Marcus Aurelius, journeying via a similar car with the inscription *sideribus recepta*, "received by the stars."[25] Like the reverses with eagles, this iconography serves to visualize the political process of deification as the figurative ferrying of the imperial *numen* to the realm of the divinities, however, a sculpture of the deceased was typically paraded in a chariot within the funerary procession, so both coin types also envisage scenes familiar to eyewitnesses of the funeral proceedings themselves. Most Roman state monuments were crowned with honorary sculptural groups and the temporary memorials were no exception. As we have seen, they were crowned with celestial chariots, which characterized the entire structures as vehicles of apotheosis.

The process of cremation (fig. 5) had long been intertwined with the notion of deification, and in his reflection on the burial practices of the early Greeks, Johnathan Musgrave has indicated that fire was believed to have the power to "start the cleansed spirit on its journey to the next world, more swiftly and dramatically than by leaving it to rot underground. It also allowed the spectator to witness for himself the soul's

departure in roaring flames and clouds of smoke."[26] The earliest recorded example of a cremation upon an elaborate architectural pyre—allegedly built to a height of sixty meters with armor and golden sculptures of mythical battle decorating its many levels—is the funeral of Hephaistion, the Macedonian general and dear friend of Alexander the Great, who was venerated as a divine hero after his astonishing immolation.[27]

At Caesar's ustrinum, the Lapis Niger complex was coopted. It epitomizes neither a tomb nor a cenotaph but a key touchstone among the scarce vestiges of permanent architecture within our archaeology of apotheosis. Despite the paucity of evidence, Barbara Levick has asserted that "Deification should imply a structure, a temple, or at least an altar at which rites could be carried out."[28] Indeed primary sources like the writings of Cassius Dio seem to imply that among the obvious requirements of a cult were a priesthood and an established site for ritual, which he called a "*bomos*."[29] While temples (fig. 6) to the imperial family have been thoroughly examined, the necessary markers of ritual spaces have received little attention as a monumental type.

In the period just before the minting of the first consecration coinage, numismatic representations of the Column of Trajan, which was completed in 113 C.E., communicated in detail the primary components of the monument, including the decorated base with an eagle at each corner, the distinctive spiral frieze, and the statue of Trajan in a heroic pose.[30] While this structure served as a tomb of the emperor and his family and did not stand at the site of his pyre, it memorialized the

Fig. 5. Sestertius of Marcus Aurelius with bust of Divus Antoninus Pius (obverse) and his four-story funeral pyre (reverse), ca. 161 C.E., D. 34.4 mm, bronze (Münzkabinett, Kunsthistorisches Museum, Vienna: RÖ 11107; photograph courtesy of the Münzkabinett, Kunsthistorisches Museum, Vienna).

Fig. 6. Aureus of Antoninus Pius with bust of Diva Faustina (obverse) and the hexastyle temple of Diva Faustina with her seated cult statue (reverse), ca. 150 C.E., D. 20.8 mm, gold (Münzkabinett, Kunsthistorisches Museum, Vienna: RÖ 11194; photograph courtesy of the Münzkabinett, Kunsthistorisches Museum, Vienna).

funerary ceremonies to a remarkable degree and embodies the combination of the column and the altar, as the pedestal, from Caesar's ustrinum.

The brilliant reading of the column of Trajan forwarded by Penelope Davies suggests that the unorthodox frieze encourages the circumambulation of the tomb in a repetition of the expiatory circling of the pyre by the troops at the funeral— the *decursio*. Indeed the reliefs of captured Dacian arms cluttered along the base coincide with the weapons placed on the pyre, the swirling narrative on the column represents Trajan's visual res gestae, his justification for deification, and the uppermost sculpture shows the emperor as finally divine.[31]

By the time Antoninus Pius had died, Lucius Verus and Marcus Aurelius elected to construct the most elaborate permanent monument at the actual site of the cremation, and coins (fig. 7) indicate that it supported a statue of Divus Antoninus and was contained within a precinct wall, an important component of the ustrinum complex according to ancient writers.[32] Significant portions of the sculpted column base survive, and the reliefs include dual sequences of the military decursio, specific mortuary rituals from the cremation. An altar, of which a part of the boundary wall survives, accompanied this large column, and consecration coins of the Antonine reign portray such walled altars (fig. 8).[33] These monumental complexes stand apart from shared dynastic mausolea, and provided sites for the cult of particular generations of the imperial family, and as with their pyres, coins perpetuate the significance of the sacred topography.

Even after the assassination of Commodus brought the adoptive line of Antoninus to an end, the funerary pyre would maintain the fiction of its continuation.[34]

When Septimius Severus took power in 193 C.E., the new emperor granted a consecratio to Pertinax, Commodus's initial Praetorian successor, and at Rome, Severus would conduct a proper imperial funeral for an effigy of Pertinax, who was never originally afforded such honors, and he would even take the cognomen Pertinax as part of his name. Severus communicated the false consecration ceremony with a pyre on a sestertius emblazoned with the image of his fictive father, the Deified Pertinax Pius Pater.[35] The funeral had developed into an imperial ritual essential to the legitimization of a successor's rule and dynastic continuity, and clearly its mediation by throngs of plebians and troops and eventually by citizens encountering the coins around the empire was necessary, just as the memory of the ustrinum was necessary for the genesis of the cult.

Simon Price posited a second-century change in commemorative politics.[36] When Pius issued images of the pyre, he bypassed the senate, which previously controlled consecration but was reluctant to elevate Hadrian after his death. Thus the emperors aligned official apotheoses directly with the ceremony of the pyre's combustion, which they oversaw and proceeded to monumentalize both in miniature and with full-size shrines.

Fig. 7. Sestertius of Marcus Aurelius with bust of Divus Antoninus Pius (obverse) and the column monument surmounted by his statue at his ustrinum (reverse), ca. 161 C.E., D. 34 mm, bronze (American Numismatic Society: 1944.100.48317; photograph courtesy of the American Numismatic Society).

Fig. 8. As of Antoninus Pius
with bust of Diva Faustina
(obverse) and a rectangular
precinct wall with a doorway
for her ustrinum altar (reverse),
ca. 140 C.E., D. 28 mm, bronze
(American Numismatic
Society: 1944.100.48974; photograph courtesy of the American Numismatic Society).

Notes

¹ Accounts of the extraordinary cremation of Julius are found
in: App. *B Civ.* 2.143–148 (White 1913, 490–501); Cic. *Phil.* 1.5
(Shackleton Bailey, Ramsey, and Manuwald 2010, 10–11); Dio
Cass. 44.50–51 (Cary and Foster 1916, 398–401); Nic. Dam.
17.48–51 (Toher 2016, 93–95); Plut. *Vit. Caes.* 68.1–3 (Perrin
1919, 602–5); and Suet. *Iul.* 1.84–86 (Rolfe 1914, 142–47). Other
incidental mentions of Caesar's funeral appear in: Cic. *Phil.* 2.91
(Shackleton Bailey, Ramsey, and Manuwald 2010, 142–43); Cicero,
Att. 14.10.1 (Shackleton Bailey 1999, 158–61); Plut. *Vit. Brut.*
20.1–7 (Perrin 1918, 168–71); Plut. *Vit. Cic.* 42.2–3 (Perrin 1919,
188–91); Plut. *Vit. Ant.* 14.3–4 (Perrin 1920, 168–71); and Quint.
Inst. 6.1.131 (Russell 2002, 32–33). The Forum location of the
event is also alluded to in the relation of his apotheosis legend: Ov.
Met. 15.840–851 (Miller 1916, 424–25) and Ov. *Fast.* 3.697–710
(Frazer and Goold 1931, 170–73).

² The Twelve Tables of ca. 450 B.C.E. laid out the regulations for
cremation and the pyre (*bustum*); Hope 2009, 154–59.

³ Koortbojian 2013, 129–32; Weinstock 1972, 353–55.

⁴ Also suggestive that the typical funerary memorial should
consist of a column, altar, and possibly a statue is the monument
to Themistocles, who had died in Thasos, in the Piraeus; Frischer
1982, 62–63.

⁵ Suet. *Iul.* 1.85 (Rolfe 1914, 144–45). An example of such an
oath offered at the shrine appears as well: Val. Max. 1.6.13 (Shackleton Bailey 2000, 76–77).

⁶ The senatorial decree did not occur until 42 B.C.E.: Koortbojian 2013, 21–22.

⁷ Caesar's wax figure appears only in one account, App. *B Civ.*
2.147 (White 1913, 498–99): "τὸ δὲ ἀνδρείκελον ἐκ μηχανῆς

ἐπεστρέφετο πάντῃ, καὶ σφαγαὶ τρεῖς καὶ εἴκοσιν ὤφθησαν ἀνά τε τὸ σῶμα πᾶν καὶ ἀνὰ τὸ πρόσωπον θηριωδῶς ἐς αὐτὸν γενόμεναι." Nonetheless, scholars have generally accepted the veracity of Appian's account, including Weinstock 1972, 352; Flower 1996, 125–26; Bodel 1999, 272; Carotta and Eickenberg 2011, 466; and Hall 2014, 135–40. Augustus dedicated the temple on 18 August 29 BCE, and its distinctive hemicycle podium contains a cylindrical altar (*bomos*): Coarelli 2007, 79; Koortbojian 2013, 41–43.

[8] The construction of the temple likely began in 140 C.E. and the dedication to Diva Faustina occurred by 144 C.E. After Antoninus's death in 161 C.E., his cult was added to this sanctuary as well: Boatwright 2011, 133–35 and Beckmann 2012, 43–48.

[9] These honors (*Hist. Aug.* Pius 6.7–8; Magie 1921, 114–15) reflect many of the supposed Roman requirements for the inception of a cult (Levick 2014, 37). As Levene (2012, 63) has discussed, however, the physical process of the funeral itself also held significant weight: "It was felt appropriate to describe an apotheosis in terms that implied that something concrete was happening in the creation of immortality." This was also the case for Divus Julius and the iconography of his commemorative coinage; see Pandey 2013, 407–15, 422.

[10] *RIC* 3 Antoninus Pius 1135–36, 1189 (Mattingly and Sydenham 1930, 164, 168). The new pyre type only appears on bronze coins of the elder Diva Faustina, although gold and silver issues of various other commemorative types are present in the series; Beckmann 2009, 205–7; 2012, 23–72.

[11] Duncan-Jones 2006, 225–28; Rowan 2011, 993–95.

[12] Faustina the elder appears in this role on *RIC* 3 Antoninus Pius 1132–34 (Mattingly and Sydenham 1930, 164). Beckmann (2012, 28–32) suggests the connections to monumental artworks.

[13] Shapiro 1983, 15–16. Regarding coins as "propaganda," see Howgego 1995, 70–73; Noreña 2011, 28–36; Elkins 2017, 4–12. The communicative potential of the coinage of Antoninus receives detailed analysis in Rowan 2013, 212–35.

[14] For later pyre coins, see Siegl 2014, 96–112. The trend of personifications on coinage is discussed by Elkins (2015, 106), and the changing burial practices are investigated by Hope (2009, 81–83).

[15] D'Ambra 2010, 289–91.

[16] Schulten 1979, 33, 75–81.

[17] *RIC* 2 Hadrian 418–419, 1051b.

[18] Beckmann 2012, 32.

[19] Davies 2004, 102–15.

[20] *RIC* 2 Trajan 743–46, 748.

[21] *RIC* 2 Trajan 751–56; Hadrian 423–26 (Mattingly and Sydenham 1926, 318, 391).

[22] Levick 2014, 35–39.

[23] Notably Herodian (Hdn. 4.2) and Dio Cassius (Dio Cass. 56.42); D'Ambra 2010, 303; and Noy 2000, 30–45.

[24] Bodel 1999, 269 and D'Ambra 2010, 292.

[25] *RIC* 3 Marcus Aurelius 1717 (Mattingly and Sydenham 1930, 350).

[26] Musgrave 1990, 272.

[27] D'Ambra 2010, 296.

[28] Blevins 2013 ; Levick 2014, 120.

[29] Dio Cass. 44.50—51; Sumi 2011, 211–12.

[30] *RIC* 2 Trajan 235, 238–39, 292–93, 307, 313, 356, 379, 579–80, 600–603, 677–80, 683 (Mattingly and Sydenham 1926, 264–92); Noreña 2011, 124–25.

[31] Davies 2000, 249; 2004, 102–15; and Frischer 1982, 73.

[32] *RIC* 3 Marcus Aurelius 439–40, 1269–72 (Mattingly and Sydenham 1930, 247, 315).

[33] *RIC* 3 Antoninus Pius 1191A–B (Mattingly and Sydenham 1930, 168); Beckmann 2012, 37–39.

[34] Kleiner and Kleiner 1978, 389–92.

[35] *RIC* 4 Septimius Severus 660C (Mattingly and Sydenham 1936, 181); Arce 2010, 310.

[36] Price 1987, 86–88.

References

Arce, J. 2010. "Roman Imperial Funerals in Effigie." In *The Emperor and Rome: Space, Representation, and Ritual*, edited by B.C. Ewald and C.F. Noreña, 309–25. Yale Classical Studies 35. Cambridge: Cambridge University Press.

Beckmann, M. 2009. "Intra-Family Die Links in the Antonine Mint at Rome." *The Numismatic Chronicle* 169:205–11.

———. 2012. *Diva Faustina: Coinage and Cult in Rome and the Provinces*. Numismatic Studies 26. New York: The American Numismatic Society.

Blevins, S.L. 2013. "Eternalizing the Emperor: Architecture, Cult, and Deification in Imperial Rome." Ph.D. Diss., Emory University.

Boatwright, M.T. 2011. "Women and Gender in the Forum Romanum." *TAPA* 141:105–41.

Bodel, J. 1999. "Death on Display: Looking at Roman Funerals." In *The Art of Ancient Spectacle*, edited by B. Bergmann and C. Kondoleon, 258–81. Studies in the History of Art 56. Washington: National Gallery of Art.

Carotta, F., and A. Eickenberg. 2011. "Liberalia Tu Accusas! Restituting the Ancient Date of Caesar's Funus." *Revue des études anciennes* 113:447–67.

Cary, E., and H.B. Foster, trans. 1916. *Dio Cassius, Roman History*. Vol. IV. LCL. Cambridge, MA: Harvard University Press.

Coarelli, F. 2007. *Rome and Environs: An Archaeological Guide*, translated by J.J. Clauss and D.P. Harmon. Berkeley: University of California Press.

D'Ambra, E. 2010. "The Imperial Funerary Pyre as a Work of Ephemeral Architecture." In *The Emperor and Rome: Space, Representation, and Ritual*, edited by B.C. Ewald and C.F. Noreña, 289–308. Yale Classical Studies 35. Cambridge: Cambridge University Press.

Davies, P.J.E. 2000. "The Phoenix and the Flames: Death, Rebirth, and the Imperial Landscape of Rome." *Mortality* 5:237–58.

———. 2004. *Death and the Emperor: Roman Imperial Funerary Monuments from Augustus to Marcus Aurelius*. Austin: University of Texas Press.

Duncan-Jones, R. 2006. "Crispina and the Coinage of the Empresses." *The Numismatic Chronicle* 166:223–28.

Elkins, N.T. 2015. *Monuments in Miniature: Architecture on Roman Coinage*. New York: American Numismatic Society.

———. 2017. *The Image of Political Power in the Reign of Nerva, AD 96–98*. Oxford: Oxford University Press.

Flower, H.I. 1996. *Ancestor Masks and Aristocratic Power in Roman Culture*. Oxford: Clarendon Press.

Frazer, J.G., and G.P. Goold, trans. 1931. *Ovid, Fasti*. LCL. Cambridge, MA: Harvard University Press.

Frischer, B. 1982. "Monumenta et Arae Honoris Virtutisque Causa: Evidence of Memorials for Roman Civic Heroes." *Bullettino della Commissione Archeologica Comunale di Roma* 88:51–86.

Hall, J. 2014. *Cicero's Use of Judicial Theater*. Ann Arbor: University of Michigan Press.

Hope, V.M. 2009. *Roman Death: The Dying and the Dead in Ancient Rome*. London: Bloomsbury.

Howgego, C. 1995. *Ancient History from Coins*. London: Routledge.

Kleiner, D.E.E., and F.S. Kleiner. 1978. "The Apotheosis of Antoninus and Faustina." *Rendiconti della Pontificia Accademia Romana di Archeologia* 51–52:389–400.

Koortbojian, M. 2013. *The Divinization of Caesar and Augustus Precedents, Consequences, Implications*. Cambridge: Cambridge University Press.

Levene, D.S. 2012. "Defining the Divine in Rome." *TAPA* 142:41–81.

Levick, B.M. 2014. *Faustina I and II Imperial: Women of the Golden Age*. Oxford: Oxford University Press.

Magie, D., trans. 1921. *Historia Augusta*. Vol. I. LCL. Cambridge, MA: Harvard University Press.

Mattingly, H. and E.A. Sydenham. 1926. *The Roman Imperial Coinage*. Vol. 2, *Vespasian to Hadrian*. London: Spink.

———. 1930. *The Roman Imperial Coinage*. Vol. 3, *Antoninus Pius to Commodus*. London: Spink.

Miller. F.J., trans. 1916. *Ovid, Metamorphoses*. Vol. II, *Books 9–15*. LCL. Cambridge, MA: Harvard University Press.

Musgrave, J. 1990. "Dust and Damn'd Oblivion: A Study of Cremation in Ancient Greece." *The Annual of the British School at Athens* 85:271–99.

Noreña, C.F. 2011. *Imperial Ideals in the Roman West: Representation, Circulation, Power.* Cambridge: Cambridge University Press.

Noy, D. 2000. "Building a Roman Funeral Pyre." *Antichthon* 34: 30–45.

Pandey, N.B. 2013. "Caesar's Comet, the Julian Star, and the Invention of Augustus." *TAPA* 143:405–49.

Perrin, B., trans. 1918. *Plutarch*, Lives. Vol. VI. LCL. Cambridge, MA: Harvard University Press.

———. 1919. *Plutarch, Lives.* Vol. VII. LCL. Cambridge, MA: Harvard University Press.

———. 1920. *Plutarch*, Lives. Vol. IX. LCL. Cambridge, MA: Harvard University Press.

Price, S.R.F. 1987. "From Noble Funerals to Divine Cult: The Consecration of Roman Emperors." In *Rituals of Royalty: Power and Ceremonial in Traditional Societies*, edited by David Cannadine and S.R.F. Price, 56–105. Cambridge: Cambridge University Press.

Rolfe, J.C., trans. 1914. *Suetonius*, Lives of the Caesars. Vol. I. LCL. Cambridge, MA: Harvard University Press.

Rowan, C. 2011. "Communicating a Consecratio: The Deification Coinage of Faustina I." In *Proceedings of the XIVth International Numismatic Congress, Glasgow 2009*, edited by N. Holmes, 991–98. Glasgow: International Numismatic Council.

———. 2013. "Imaging the Golden Age: The Coinage of Antoninus Pius." *Papers of the British School at Rome* 81:211–46.

Russell, D.A. 2002. *Quintilian*, The Orator's Education. Vol. III, Books 6–8. LCL. Cambridge, MA: Harvard University Press.

Schulten, P.N. 1979. *Die Typologie der römischen Konsekrationsprägungen.* Frankfurt: Numismatischer Verlag Schulten.

Shackleton Bailey, D.R, trans. 1999. *Cicero*, Letters to Atticus. Vol. IV. LCL. Cambridge, MA: Harvard University Press.

———, trans. 2000. *Valerius Maximus, Memorable Doings and Sayings.* Vol. I. LCL. Cambridge, MA: Harvard University Press.

Shackleton Bailey, D.R., J.T. Ramsey, and G. Manuwald, eds. and trans. 2010. *Cicero, Philippics 1–6.* LCL. Cambridge, MA: Harvard University Press.

Shapiro, H.A. 1983. "'Hêrôs Theos': The Death and Apotheosis of Herakles." *CW* 77:7–18.

Siegl, K. 2014. "Scheiterhaufendarstellungen auf römischen Konsekrationsprägungen." *Schweizerische Numismatische Rundschau* 93:91–130.

Sumi, G.S. 2011. "Topography and Ideology: Caesar's Monument and the Aedes Divi Iulii in Augustan Rome." CQ 61: 205–19.

Toher, M., trans. 2016. *Nicolaus of Damascus*, The Life of Augustus *and* The Autobiography. Cambridge: Cambridge University Press.

Weinstock, S. 1972. *Divus Julius*. Oxford: Oxford University Press.

White, H., trans. 1913. *Appian*, Roman History. Vol. 3, *The Civil Wars*. LCL. Cambridge, MA: Harvard University Press.

Art Appropriation on the Coins of Fausta Flavia Maxima

Rosa Maria Motta

Abstract

Roman imperial coin types drew from a highly developed visual language of imperial ideology and have been widely studied within that context. This paper presents Fausta's coins in the narrower context of Constantine's deliberate attempt to evoke Rome's imperial past. The replication of Faustina's (wife of Marcus Aurelius) physiognomical style and coin type attempts to transfer Faustina's dignity, nobility, and worthiness to Fausta, the new AUGUSTA. Moreover, in circulating to far-flung places, Fausta's coins become an effective tool for spreading Constantine's promise of prosperity throughout the newly unified Roman empire. The young Faustina look-alike empress and her children inspired confidence that the prosperity of the past would continue in the future.

> "Your mother's ancestry was so distinguished; her personal beauty and nobility of character were such that it would be hard to find her match among women. [...] No other woman had been the sister, mother, wife, and daughter of kings."[1]

THE CONCEPT OF ART APPROPRIATION AND ART DESPOLIA-tion is based on words from the field of art history terminology, where appropriation is defined as "the practice of artists using preexisting objects or images in their art with little transformation of the original,"[2] and despoliation refers mostly to the reuse of parts (*spolia*) of architectural constructions taken or appropriated from demolished buildings. The idea of reuse seems to fit rather well with the modern fascination for recycling and reusing, but if the notion is new, the practice of reusing parts of buildings or artifacts is quite old. Examples of reused material can already be found on the Athenian Acropolis, for instance, where grave monuments were taken down and reused by the Athenians to rebuild their city wall in 479 B.C.E.[3] The most accelerated progress of both despoliation and appropriation, however, was enacted in the early fourth century C.E. by Constantine the Great. His architects used *spolia* from monuments of Trajan, Hadrian, and Marcus Aurelius on two important monuments, the Lateran Basilica and the triumphal arch, built in Rome between 312–315 C.E.

The arch's reused *spolia* were originally designed to celebrate the victories and virtues of Trajan, Hadrian, and Marcus Aurelius; as a consequence, these spolia have prompted scholars, starting with Hans Peter L'Orange (*Der spätantike Bildschmuck des Konstantinsbogens*, 1939), to interpret the appropriation as Constantine's conscious attempt to claim the legitimacy of his predecessors. By replacing their features with his own on those *spolia*, Constantine literally integrated himself into their world, appropriating the celebration of their deeds as his own.[4] Moreover, since the arch was built to celebrate Constantine's victory over Maxentius, the use of the reliefs of the older emperors has been analyzed in the context of Constantine's intended political assertion. The appropriation represents Constantine's conscious hope that the qualities of the appropriated objects would be transferred to him.[5] He hoped, in other words, that the reused reliefs of former emperors would evoke early Roman traditions in the eyes of the viewers, placing him in the midst of a revered line of Roman emperors.

While Constantine's Arch has been analyzed within the ideological context of art appropriation, his numismatic repertoire has never been examined within that same setting. This paper argues that the same notion can be extended to the numismatic portraits of Fausta, Constantine's wife. Fausta's numismatic portraiture (No. 1) seems deliberately to accentuate the likeness of the young empress with the numismatic images of Faustina the Younger, wife of Marcus Aurelius (No. 2). Fausta's regular profile with large eyes and heavy eyelids and the classical hairstyle of wavy hair tied in a bun on the back of her neck bears a striking resemblance to Faustina, whose name Fausta's recalls.

Fausta as Empress

Fausta's entrance into public life occurred with her marriage to Constantine in April 307, when she was possibly as young as seventeen. The ceremony took place in a period of political turmoil, marked by the premature death of Constantius

No. 1: Fausta, AU Solidus; 4.41 gr; 324–325 C.E., Nicodemia. *RIC* 7 77.
OBV: Bust of Fausta, draped, wearing imperial mantle, head, with hair waved and
tied back in bun, right. FLAV MAX FAVSTA AVG.
REV: Fausta, veiled, draped, standing front, head left, holding two children, one in
each arm. SALVS REIPVBLICAE; Ex: SMN.

No. 2: Faustina II; AU Aureus, 7.26 gr; 161–176 C.E.; Rome; *RIC* 3 692.
OBV: Bust of Faustina II, draped, right, hair waved and fastened in bun, low at back.
FAVSTINA AVGVSTA.
REV: Juno, draped, standing front, head left, holding child on left arm and extending
right hand downwards; at her sides, two children, both facing left and raising right
hands. IVNONI LVCINAE.

Chlorus, Constantine's father and the Western Augustus (in the middle of 306) and the conflicts that followed. After the death of Severus—who had been Caesar under Constantius—Maximian, father of Fausta, offered the hand of his daughter in marriage to Constantine, son of Constantius Chlorus and self-proclaimed Augustus in order to strengthen his position.[6] The panegyric pronounced at the wedding ceremony presents the union as a divine marriage that would make eternal the descendants of Maximian, while also emphasizing the dynastic prospects of Constantine.[7]

A first mention of Fausta's beauty as a young girl is offered in a panegyric that describes a fresco belonging to the imperial residence of Aquileia.[8] In the painting, the young Fausta is portrayed as offering a gift to Constantine, as if Maximian, who ordered the fresco, had already predicted the union between his daughter and Constantine. There is however, no trace of this fresco, nor any other confirmed portraits of Fausta. The bust at the Louvre (Inv. MA4881), which Richard Delbrück wanted to identify as the face of young Fausta most likely belongs to an earlier age.[9] Another portrait of a possible young Fausta was found behind the Tempio d'Ercole in Ostia and is now at the Museo Ostiense (Inv. 80), but has not been confirmed. A more likely candidate is a draped statue of the first half of the fourth century C.E., found in 1939 in the seat of the *Collegio degli Augustali* of Ostia and now housed at the Museo Ostiense (Inv. 22). The statue was first identified by Calza as Faustina, wife of Marcus Aurelius. Later, however, she redated the statue to 320–340 C.E. and identified the statue with Fausta.[10] This specific portrait shows a notable affinity with the numismatic effigies of Fausta. The firm and delicately round oval of her face, the calm expression of her eyes with lowered eyelids, and the classical hairstyle similar to those of the Antonine women, seem to confirm that the statue represents Fausta—the classical beauty described by Julian.[11] Finally, a marble head, presumed to be Fausta, was acquired by the Spurlock Museum of World Culture in Illinois in 1982 (Inv. 1982.07.0001), but it has never been published.

The Roman system brought with it an emphasis on the female members of the imperial house—the emperors were at the center of the political game, but their wives and daughters occupied important positions for the maintenance and, mainly, perpetuation of the imperial house.[12] Some earlier empresses took advantage of their proximity to the center of power to directly interfere in the political game, as in the cases of Livia (58 B.C.E.–29 C.E.), wife of Octavian (r. 27 B.C.E.–14 C.E.); Julia Domna, wife of Septimius Severus (r. 193–211 C.E.) and mother of Caracalla (r. 198–217 C.E.); and Helena, mother of Constantine (r. 306–337 C.E.).[13] Although a Roman empress did not have an officially defined role, she assumed various relevant public roles. Primarily, it was up to the emperor's wife to accompany him to various religious ceremonies, to receive senators, and in the Late Empire, also bishops, in addition to often being the closest confidant to the ruler. The imperial house was both a public space, as a residence of the sovereign, and private one, since the members of the imperial family resided there. As Mary Nash reminds us, the private sphere belonged to women, and since it was almost impossible to separate the public and the private spaces in the imperial house, there is a good possibility that an imperial woman's authority in court increased, especially once she acquired the title of *Augusta*—an official position at the side of the emperor.[14]

From numismatic and epigraphic material, we can assess that the women of Constantine's court were especially influential and might even have impacted aspects of the emperors' policies. After he became the sole emperor in 324 C.E., for instance, he honored both his wife and, though rare in Roman history, his mother with the title of *Augusta*, perhaps in symbolically sharing his power with them. After the death of Fausta, Helena played a decisive role in stimulating the construction of churches in the Holy Land, in addition to achieving eminence in her role as queen mother and *progenetrix* of the imperial dynasty.[15] Constantine's three daughters also played an important role in relations between Constantine and the bishops, and later became wives or mothers of emperors. Numismatic representations of these women are plentiful and dispersed throughout the empire, attesting to their importance.

Fausta's Coins

Numismatic images of imperial women, which were rare in the early period of the empire, peaked with Marcus Aurelius, who minted twenty-two different reverse types for his wife Faustina, and continued to grow with later emperors. Septimius Severus, for instance, minted twenty-five reverse types for his wife Julia Domna.[16] The tetrarchic period, with its emphasis on unity and uniformity, had started a decline on the variety of typology,[17] but the rise of Constantine as a sole ruler brought back a multiplicity of types. Fausta's coin iconography must be analyzed in the context of Constantine's assertion of power and his emphasis on traditions and on the remembrance of traditional values and images.

The first numismatic issue with Fausta's portrait is dated from the time of the wedding. A half *argenteus* was coined in the name of FAUSTAE NOBILISSIMAE FEMINAE in Trier in 307 right around the date of the wedding (No. 3). The reverse of this coin depicts Venus, sitting and displaying a symbol of power—the *orbis terrarum*, and the palm of victory. The numismatic representation of Venus points to Fausta's important role in sharing in the character of the imperial household by incapsulating Roman virtues and the prospects of a prospering dynasty. The coin seems to replicate Faustina the Younger's *Venus Felix* type, where Venus is also sitting and holding the Three Graces in her extended right hand and transverse scepter in her left hand (No. 4). The reuse of the older *Venus-Felix* type iconography on Fausta's first coin emphasizes how important it was for Constantine to create a visual connection between himself and his wife and their predecessors. Venus was a goddess of deep national resonance for the Romans, and her presence on Fausta's first coin presents an ideology of dynastic stability in times of unrest.

After the defeat of his rival Licinius in 324 C.E. and the unification of the empire under him as the sole Augustus, Constantine bestowed the title of Augusta on his wife, and a medallion with the new title was issued to commemorate the occasion (No. 5). The obverse again portrays the classical, Faustina-style image; the reverse depicts Fausta seated on a throne set on platform and decorated with garlands, and seems to hail Fausta's motherhood. The princess is in fact holding a child in her lap, possibly Constans who was born in 323. Fausta also appears on the reverse of Crispus's medallion minted in 324 C.E. (No. 6). Wearing her imperial mantle, she stands with both hands placed on the shoulders of Crispus and Constantine II, who are facing each other and clasping their right hands. Fausta's maternal role as a peacemaker is clear as she strives to restore harmony between her son and

stepson.

No. 3: Fausta; AR Half Argenteus (1.2g); ca. 307 C.E. Trier. *RIC* 6 756
OBV: Portrait of Fausta, left, wavy hair tied in a high bun. FAVSTAE NOBILIS-
SIMAE FEMINAE.
REV: A seated Venus left, holding palm of victory in left hand, and the *orbis terrarum*
in right hand. VENVS FELIX; Ex: TR.

No. 4: Faustina II, AU Denarius; 3.53 gr; 161–176 C.E.; Rome; *RIC* 3 731
OBV: Bust of Faustina II, draped, right. FAVSTINA AVGVSTA.
REV: Venus seated left, holding Victory in extended right hand and vertical scepter
in left hand. VENVS FELIX.

No. 5: Fausta AU Medallion; 8.8 gr; 324 C.E.; Trier. *RIC* 7 443.
OBV: Bust of Fausta, right, draped, wearing imperial mantle, head, with hair waved and tied back in bun. FLAVIA MAXIMA FAVSTA AVGVSTA
REV: Fausta, draped, nimbate, seated facing front on throne, set on platform decorated with garlands, holding child in lap: to left, *Felicitas*, draped, standing right, holding caduceus; to right *Pietas* standing right; on either side of platform, Genius with wreath. PIETAS AVGVSTAE. Ex: PTR.

No. 6. Crispus AU medallion; 8.72 gr.; 324 C.E.; Trier; *RIC* 7 442.
OBV: Bust of Crispus, wearing imperial mantle, holding scepter surmounted by eagle in right hand, head, laureate, left. FL IVL CRISPVS NOB CAES.
REV: Fausta, wearing imperial mantle, standing center facing front, with both hands places on shoulders of Crispus, left, and Constantine II, right, both togate, facing each other, and clasping right hands. FELIX PROGENIES CONSTANTINI AVG.

Fausta's *Spes*-type coins minted in 326 C.E. (No. 7) offer an iconography that differs from the Roman conventional representation of *Spes*. As the personification of hope, *Spes* was almost invariably depicted on coins as a young woman holding a flower in her extended right hand, while the left hand raises a fold of her dress. On Fausta's coins, however, the young woman seems to be the empress herself, holding her two infant sons close to her chest in a type that evokes Faustina's *Fecunditas*-type coins (No. 8). The honorific portraits on the obverses of both Faustina's and Fausta's coins have similarities. Fausta's demeanor, and especially her hair, waved and coiled in a small bun at the lower back of the head, resemble Faustina's. Both princesses are in fact depicted with a version of the *Scheitelzopf*—a coiffure in which the hair is parted in the center, waved, and brought into a bun, low on the nape of the neck.[18] Fausta's facial features, regular, with a low forehead, but with an aquiline nose and a small pointed chin, are less perfectly symmetrical than those of Faustina. The reverse, however, which depicts Fausta holding two children close to her chest, more closely evokes Faustina's *fecunditas* type coins. The Antonine princess is depicted holding two small babies in her arms with a pair of young children huddling close on either side and with the legend, FECVND(ITATI) AVGVSTAE; Fausta's legend, SPES REI PUBLICAE acknowledges that Hope has manifested itself in the princess' ability to mother the next emperors. The same iconography appears on Fausta's *Salus*-type coins (No. 1), again highlighting the importance of her motherhood for the safety of the empire.

The examination of the numismatic representation of both Faustina and Fausta invites a consideration of who was responsible for the designs and motifs on their coinage. As part of the ongoing discussion of whether an emperor was responsible for the selection of his coin types, one must agree with William Metcalf that coin designs "had to flatter the emperor and be subject to his approval."[19] Since coins were likely seen by the inhabitants of the empire as the product and responsibility of the emperor himself, it is reasonable to consider the coinage of a reign a composite portrait of the ruler as he liked to see himself, perhaps "intended not as publicity but for internal, domestic, palace consumption."[20] As it turns out, many writers often attribute the selection of types to the emperors themselves. Eusebius, for instance, argues that

No. 7: Fausta, AU Solidus, 324–325 C.E.; Sirmium; *RIC* 7 178.
OBV: Draped bust, right. FLAV MAX-FAVSTA AVG.
REV: Empress standing, facing r, holding two infants in her arms. SPES REI-PVBLICAE. Ex: SIRM.

No. 8: Faustina II, Sestertius, AE, 27.05 gr., 161–176 C.E.; Rome. *RIC* 3 1635.
OBV: Bust of Faustina II, draped, right. FAUSTINA AUGUSTA.
REV: Fecunditas standing facing, head left, holding child in each arm; by her side, two children standing left and right, and raising left and right arms. FECVND AVGVS-TAE.

Constantine was directly responsible for his depiction in a posture of prayer.[21] The potential role of the imperial women in the selection of coin types is more difficult to prove, given the absence of literary evidence. But this very absence may be significant: the public images of empresses generated by their coinage likely conformed to and enhanced the public ideology of their husbands.

In her book, *Die Frauen am Hofe Trajans*, Hildegard Temporini investigated the impact of imperial women on the imagery and propaganda of Trajan's rule and proved that Trajan's Roman coinage had a new focus on the female members of his family because the public image of the Ulpian family—subservient and utterly devoted to the emperor—was linked with the promotion of Trajan's legitimacy.[22] The same can clearly be said about Constantine, whose coinage was meant to be a demonstration of the monarchical character of his reign. His new dynasty would last beyond the emperor's death, thus securing internal peace to the Roman nation. Consequently, nearly all reverses of Fausta's coins display her in the role of a mother—a crucial factor for the relevance of Fausta in her husband's reign.

Faustina's reign as *Augusta* lasted nearly 30 years, from 147 C.E., after the birth of her first child, until her death in 175 C.E., and the overarching memory of her fecundity, after a long line of childless emperors, must have lasted until the time of Constantine. Marcus Aurelius's devotion to his wife and his grief over her loss in 175 C.E. were widely known past Faustina's times. For instance, Cassius Dio tells that on the eve of his wedding to Julia Domna, Septimius Severus had a dream in which the empress Faustina herself "prepared their nuptial chamber in the temple of Venus near the palace."[23] By the time of Diocletian (r. 284–305 C.E.), Marcus Aurelius had been idealized and worshipped as a divinity, and Diocletian himself is said to have desired, "to be such a one as Marcus in life and gentleness."[24] Finally, Julian the Apostate (r. 361–363 C.E.) praised Fausta's beauty and ancestry in his panegyric in honor of emperor Constantius and wrote in his *Letter to Themistius* of his admiration for Marcus Aurelius's "perfect virtues."[25]

Given the widespread favorable reputation of Marcus Aurelius and his wife during the reign of Constantine's predecessor and successor, it is reasonable to assume that Constantine himself held Marcus Aurelius in high esteem, desiring to model his reign after the successful older emperor. Marcus Aurelius's wife, Faustina, would as a consequence be a model for the young empress. By modeling Fausta's numismatic images on Faustina's, Constantine—or Fausta herself—enhanced the emperor's public image and ideology.

Fausta's reign as Augusta lasted only two years, as she met a tragic end in 326 C.E. at the prime of her life. No official explanation was ever given following the incident, but the circumstances of her death or possible execution have been debated over the centuries, with the only certainty being that she died in the bath. Constantine seems to have ordered the *damnatio memoriae* of his wife with the result that no contemporary source records details of her fate.[26] Eusebius, for instance, mentions neither Fausta nor Crispus (who was also killed) in his *Vita Constantini*; significantly, her three sons, once in power, never revoked this order. As a consequence of the *damnatio memoriae*, no statue of the empress has been definitely identified, and no coins with her image were minted after her death.

While Constantine despoiled ancient monuments, and cut his face in Marcus Aurelius's place, perhaps to acquire his virtues, Fausta was modeled as Faustina in her numismatic portraiture. Perhaps Constantine hoped that she also would acquire Faustina's qualities. As mentioned, Fausta's coins especially seem to focus on Faustina's *Fecunditas* type coins, perhaps to point out that, just like Faustina, who was one of the most fecund Roman empresses, she too had been successful in giving birth to five children. And perhaps, just like Marcus Aurelius, Constantine also envisioned his wife's motherhood as providential. However, in contrast to Faustina who was portrayed as an ancestress surrounded by her surviving children (No. 2), Fausta is always holding a pair of infants at her breasts; the children are portrayed in an upright sitting position with their outward arms raised as if nursing. Clearly, Constantine and his family are promoting a symbolism of Fausta as a *dea nutrix*.[27]

The circulation of coinage in the Roman Empire allowed a flow of specific information that could shape public opinion at both national and transnational levels. The debate on deliberation and intent on coin iconography, however, is open to various interpretations. For some scholars, for instance, Roman coins were organs of information that served a propagandist purpose;[28] for others, speaking of propaganda in

Roman times is anachronistic.[29] More recently, Meadows and Williams have added to the debate by viewing the imagery of Roman coins as "small-scale but widely-circulating monuments … intended to promote ideas of continuity and tradition."[30]

The debate on deliberation and intent on coin iconography is evidently unresolved. Nevertheless, it is reasonable to establishes a connection between forms and content of those images and expressions of ideology, for example, glorification of state and ruler, war and triumph. Of additional importance on Roman coins is the use of personification of virtues (e.g., *Fecunditas* on Faustina's coin; *Spes* and *Salus* on Fausta's). The abstract symbols that came to denote the virtues developed into a complex numismatic visual language that operated on a collective unconscious.[31] Hence, the image of the empress and her children on Fausta's coin must have evoked the joys of motherhood and the stability of the dynasty. Finally, inscriptions, which carried written messages throughout the empire, were an important component of the Roman imperial typology. The title Augusta, for instance, inscribed on both Faustina's and Fausta's coins, was a clear recognition of the unique value of their coins as official documents that reflected the new role of both empresses.

The appropriation and reuse of Faustina's imagery on Fausta's coins throughout the Roman Empire achieved several goals: (1) it placed Constantine's new imperial family in the pantheon of successful Roman rulers and their families; (2) it pointed the viewers to a renewed era of prosperity, similar to the one enjoyed under Marcus Aurelius; and (3) it inspired the confidence that such prosperity would continue for as long as Constantine's dynasty endured. Fausta's children in her arms, like the children on Faustina's *Fecunditas* type coin, represented not only the future of the dynasty, but the sustainability of Rome itself within the new era initiated by Constantine.

Notes

[1] Julian the Apostate, *Panegyric in Honour of Emperor Constantius.*

[2] Lack 2008, 20–21.

[3] Kousser 2009, 266–67. Several hypotheses have been brought forward for the reworking and reuse of grave monuments. According to Keesling (1999), the faces of several artifacts were damaged

to deprive them of "power" before incorporating them into the wall (518).

⁴ L'Orange writes, "Is it an accident that he [Constantine] is represented in image-cycles, well known to all Romans, of just these three rulers? Doesn't he [...] appear before their eyes as Novus Trajanus, Novus Hadrianus, Novus Marcus, i.e., a guarantor of the Saeculum Aureum?" (L'Orange and Gerkan 1978, 191). Several additional studies have, of course, discussed *spolia*, including articles by Elsner (2000) and Kinney (1995, 1997, 2012). More recently, Brilliant and Kinney (2016) published a collection of essays that discuss how the reuse of materials may have different meanings for archaeologists than for art historians.

⁵ Fabricius Hansen 2003, 263.

⁶ Barnes 1973, 30.

⁷ Plin. *Pan.* 7.7.1–3 by an anonymous author, delivered at the wedding ceremony traditionally dated to late April or early May 31 307 C.E.

⁸ Plin. *Pan.* 7.6.2–3. "The fresco of the palace of Aquileia ... in which a little girl whose divine beauty already commanded respect, but still unable to carry her weight, holds a glittering helmet of gold and precious stones in her hands and offers it to you, Constantine ..."

⁹ Delbrück 1978, 166. The author claims that the head looks like that of a fourteen-year old southern girl, ("Das dargerstellte Alter wird bei einem *südlichen* Madchen etwa 14 Jaher betragen"), identifiable with Fausta.

¹⁰ Calza (De Chirico) 1941, 216–46. See also McFadden 2013, 83–114.

¹¹ Calza 1950, 201.

¹² Hillard 1992, 38–39. See also Pomeroy 1987.

¹³ Hillard 1992, 38–39.

¹⁴ Nash 1982, 32. For more on the role of imperial women, see Burns 2007.

¹⁵ Bowder 1978, 55–64. Helena's importance as *genetrix* can also be attested by the eight extant inscriptions dedicated to her. On the inscription found near the Basilica of S. Croce, Helena is called grandmother of the Caesars. See Drijvers 1992, 49.

¹⁶ Horster 2007, 292.

¹⁷ Howgego 1995, 69; See also Abdy 2012, 584–600.

¹⁸ For Fausta's numismatic portrait typology, see Calza 1972, 249; Kleiner 1992, 443.

¹⁹ Metcalf 2006, 42. See also Ando 2013, 216; Duncan 2005, 462–63.

²⁰ Levik 1982, 108.

²¹ Euseb. *Vit. Const.* 3.47.2.

²² Temporini 1979, 10–18. For more on Pliny's panegyric on the Ulpian family, see Roche 2002, 41–60.

²³ Cass. Dio, *Historia Romana*, 74.3.

[24] *Historia Augusta, Vita Marci*, 19.12.

[25] Julian the Apostate, *Letter to Themistius*, 2:199–237. For the panegyric see n. 1.

[26] Woods (1998) argues that she died while being forced to terminate an illegitimate pregnancy. Silva (2010) argues that she created a false suspicion about Crispus and that once discovered, Constantin ordered Fausta to enter the *caldarium* of the imperial palace, in which the water was superheated causing her to drown.

[27] Vanderspoel and Mann 2002, 350.

[28] Sutherland et al. 1984; Grant 1952.

[29] Levick 1982, 104–16. See also Crawford 1983, 47–64.

[30] Meadows and Williams 2007, 43. The fact that the Latin word, *monumentum*, has the same root as *moneta* and *moneo* (to remind/ suggest) implies, according to the authors, that a *monumentum* served as a means of bringing something or someone to people's mind. So, anything done to preserve the memory is a *monumentum* (p. 41).

[31] Hölscher 1980, 265–321. Coin iconography as part of Roman art can be compared with the forms of Roman literature and with the language of art discussed by Hölscher.

References

Abdy, R. 2012. "Tetrarchy and the House of Constantine." In *The Oxford Handbook of Greek and Roman Coinage*, edited by William E. Metcalf, 584–600. Oxford: Oxford University Press.

Ando, C. 2013. *Imperial Ideology and Provincial Loyalty in the Roman Empire*. Berkeley: University of California Press.

Barnes, T.D. 1973. "Lactantius and Constantine." *JRS* 63:29–46.

Brilliant, R., and D. Kinney, eds. 2016. *Reuse Value: Spolia and Appropriation in Art and Architecture from Constantine to Sherrie Levine*. New York: Routledge.

Bowder, D. 1978. *The Age of Constantine and Julian*. London: Elek.

Burns, J. 2007. *Great Women of Imperial Rome: Mothers and Wives of the Caesars*. London: Routledge.

Cassius Dio. 1914–1927. *Historia Romana*, rev. ed., translated by Earnest Cary. LCL. Cambridge, MA: Harvard University Press.

Calza, R. 1950. "Statua iconica femminile da Ostia." *Bollettino d'arte* 35–36:201–7.

——— (De Chirico). 1941. "Ostia. Sculture Provenienti dall'Edicio degli Augustali." In *Notizie degli Scavi di Antich- ità*, 234–37. Rome: Accademia nazionale dei Lincei.

———. 1972. *Iconografia Romana Imperiale da Carausio a Giuliano*. Rome: L'Erma di Bretschneider.

Crawford, M. 1983. "Roman Imperial Coin Types and the Formation of Public Opinion." In *Studies in Numismatic Method Presented to Philip Grierson*, edited by C.N. Brooke, B. Stewart, and J. Pollard, 47–64. Cambridge: Cambridge University Press.

Delbrück, R. 1978. *Spätantike Kaiserporträts von Constantinus Magnus bis zum Ende des Westreichs*. Berlin: Walter de Gruyter. Repr. of 1933 edition.

Drijvers, J.W. 1992. *Helena Augusta*. Leiden: E. J. Brill.

Duncan, R.P. 2005. "Implications of Roman Coinage: Debates and Differences." *Klio* 87:459–87.

Elsner, J. 2000. "From the Culture of Spolia to the Cult of Relics: The Arch of Constantine and the Genesis of Late Antique Forms." *Papers of the British School at Rome* 68:149–84.

Eusebius. 2015. *Life of Constantine*. New York: Scriptura.

Fabricius Hansen, M. 2003. *The Eloquence of Appropriation: Prolegomena to an Understanding of Spolia in Early Christian Rome*. Rome: L'Erma di Bretschneider.

Grant, M. 1952. "Roman Coins as Propaganda." *Archaeology* 5.2: 79–85.

Hillard, T. 1992. "On the Stage, Behind the Curtains." In *Stereotypes of Women in Power*, edited by B. Garlick, S. Dixon, and P. Allen, 37–64. Westport, CT: Greenwood Press.

Hölscher, T. 1980. "Die Geschichtsauffassung in der Römischen Repräsentationskunst." *JdI* 95:265–321.

Horster, M. 2007. "The Emperor's Family on Coins." In *Crisis and the Roman Empire*, edited by O. Hekster, G. Kleijn, and D. Slootjes, 291–310. Leiden: E. J. Brill.

Howgego, C. 1995. *Ancient History from Coins*. London: Routledge.

Julian the Apostate. 1913. *Letter to Themistius. Works*. Vol. 2, translated by Wilmer Cave Wright, 199–237. LCL 13. London: Heinemann.

———. 1913. *Panegyric in Honour of Constantius. Works*. Vol. 1, translated by Wilmer Cave Wright, 2–127. LCL 13. London: Heinemann.

Keesling, C. 1999. "Endoios's Painting from the Themistoklean Wall: A Reconstruction." *Hesperia* 68.4:509–48.

Kinney, D. 1995. "Rape or Restitution of the Past? Interpreting Spolia." In *The Art of Interpreting*, edited by S.C. Scott, 52–67. University Park, PA: Pennsylvania State University Press.

———. 1997. "Spolia. 'Damnatio' and 'Renovatio Memoriae.'" *Memoirs of the American Academy in Rome* 42:117–48.

———. 2012. "Instances of Appropriation in Late Roman and Early Christian Art." *Essays in Medieval Studies* 28:1–22.

Kleiner, D. 1992. *Roman Sculpture*. New Haven: Yale University Press.

Kousser, R. 2009. "Destruction and Memory on the Athenian Acropolis." *The Art Bulletin* 91.3:263–82.

Lack, J. 2008. *The Tate Guide to Modern Art Term*. London: Tate.

Levick, B. 1982. "Propaganda and the Imperial Coinage." *Antichthon* 16:104–16.

L'Orange, H.P., and A. von Gerkan. 1978. *Der Spätantike Bildschmuck des Konstantinsbogens*. Berlin: Walter de Gruyter.

McFadden, S. 2013. "A Constantinian Image Program in Rome Rediscovered: The Late Antique Megalographia from the So-called 'Domus Faustae.'" *Memoirs of the American Academy in Rome* 58:83–114.

Meadows, A., and J. Williams. 2007. "Coinage." In *The Edinburgh Companion to Ancient Greece and Rome*, edited by E. Bispham, T. Harrison, and B. Sparks, 173–82. Edinburgh: Edinburgh University Press.

Metcalf, W.E. 2006. "Roman Imperial Numismatics" in *A Companion to the Roman Empire* edited by D.S. Potter, 35–44. Malden, MA: Blackwell.

Nash, M. 1982. "Desde la Invisibilidad a la Presencia de la Mujer en la Historia." In *Nuevas Perspectivas sobre la Mujer: Actas de las Primeras Jornadas de Investigación Interdisciplinaria* edited by María Angeles Durán, 19–37. Madrid: Universidad Autonoma.

Pomeroy, S. 1987. *Diosas, Rameras, Esposas y Esclavas*. Madrid: Akal.

Roche, P. 2002. "The Public Image of Trajan's Family." *CP* 97.1:41–60.

Silva, D. 2010. "FLAVIA MAXIMA FAVSTA AVGVSTA: Possibilidades e limites de uma biografia histórica." *Revista do Museu de Arqueologia e Etnologia* 20:277–92.

Sutherland, C. et al. 1984. *The Roman Imperial Coinage*. Vol. 7, *Constantine and Licinius*. London: Spink & Sons.

Temporini, H. 1979. *Die Frauen am Hofe Trajans: Ein Beitrag zur Stellung der Augustae im Principat*. Berlin: Walter de Gruyter.

Vanderspoel, J., and M. Mann. 2002. "The Empress Fausta as Romano-Celtic Dea Nutrix." *The Numismatic Chronicle* 162:350–55.

Woods, D. 1998. "On the Death of the Empress Fausta." *Greece & Rome* 45.1:70–86.